The Picture Book of
BODY
LANGUAGE

Anna Jaskolka trained as an actress at East 15 Drama School in London, where she later helped to develop and encourage the Stanislavsky Method School of acting. She went on to lead workshops centring on human observation, examining the way in which emotion manifests within the body and is the impetus for movement. Her interest in the workings of the human mind and a desire to develop her performance skills led her to study hypnotherapy. As an actor she has worked extensively in film, television and theatre, and she is currently touring worldwide with a one-woman show written by herself, *Magic Moments*. Her other books include *Teen Dreams and What They Mean*. Anna has one son and lives in Essex with her husband, four dogs, four cats, three horses and a flock of geese, ducks and hens.

The Picture Book of
BODY
LANGUAGE

The only language in which people can't lie

Anna Jaskolka

foulsham
LONDON • NEW YORK • TORONTO • SYDNEY

foulsham

Capital Point, 33 Bath Road, Slough, Berkshire, SL1 3UF, England

Foulsham books can be found in all good bookshops and direct from www.foulsham.com

ISBN 978-0-572-03554-9

Copyright © 2011 Anna Jaskolka

Text previously published as *How to Read and Use Body Language*

Picture research by Jo St Mart

Cover photographs reproduced with kind permission from Powerstock

A CIP record for this book is available from the British Library.

The moral right of the author has been asserted.

Printed and bound in Great Britain by Martins the Printers Ltd

Contents

Introduction

I have always been intrigued by the way people interact and communicate with each other, and people-watching has always been a hobby of mine. Our mannerisms and body signals are there for all to see, yet often we do not fully appreciate that our non-verbal communication greatly affects both the way we perceive others and the way we are perceived ourselves.

My interest in body language was piqued during my early childhood years. I have vivid recollections of my family and friends ritually passing dreary, wet Sunday afternoons huddled together around a table, eating, drinking and exchanging gossip, but for the most part engaged in the serious business of playing poker. My father is Polish, and poker was a popular pastime in his native land. He was keen to re-establish the card game in his new environment when he moved to England.

A hush would descend over the house as the curtains were drawn to set the scene for the ensuing battle. Then the cards would appear. I would be allowed into the hallowed room only if I discreetly blended into the floral-patterned wallpaper and didn't make a sound. My eyes would be transfixed as the men began to stack their hard-earned money on the table and the serious game of poker commenced.

Crouched behind my father's well-worn chair, I became a silent witness to this family ritual, and a captivated voyeur of each participant's every move and grimace. These hardened poker players would huff, puff and try to bluff their way to victory, their faces often a picture of concentration.[1] Polish vodka would flow freely as the games were won and lost – wins celebrated and sorrows drowned.

My attention was inexorably drawn towards the players' gestures, expressions and posture during this predominantly silent combat, and I sat mesmerised, trying to read their every thought and move. Each twitch, shift of position, smile, scratch and sigh belied the silent desire to express an emotion or thought.[2] Over time I became increasingly successful at working out who had the winning hand and who was trying to bluff with an inferior hand. As I studied the players' attempts to maintain the

3

4

5

classic 'poker face', I began to realise that this was a very difficult feat to achieve – a near impossibility in fact.

When a thought passes though a person's mind, the body's natural response is to express it immediately. The rare sight of four aces in a hand of poker would evoke a strong emotional response in anyone. Simply put, you would want to whoop with delight and beam your biggest smile, but, of course, if you did so during a game you would never be a successful poker player![3] The reverse, of course, is also true.[4] To conceal these instinctive reactions takes immense physical and mental control. Even when self-control is apparently mastered effectively to the untrained eye, a competent student of body language can still spot some subtle tell-tale signs.

Let's imagine that an experienced player is comfortably able to keep virtually all his physical movements under conscious control. Even here, there are still some reflexes that he will not be able to suppress: in particular, movements of the pupils. At the sight of a good hand of cards, adrenalin immediately starts to pump through the body and the pupils automatically dilate. This reaction cannot be prevented. Other gestures may be habitual, such as touching the mouth in response to a particular stimulus.[5]

American films often show card players wearing sunglasses in a darkened casino when they are playing serious poker. This is not just about trying to look cool. In fact, as every seasoned player knows, this practice helps to conceal the players' eyes, so that they will not give themselves away if they are dealt a fantastic hand of cards.

My fascination with people-watching led me to pursue a career as an actress. At drama school I was encouraged to study the subtleties and complexity of non-verbal communication in greater depth. I learnt how to maximise the effectiveness of my body language, an essential skill if an actor is to play a character convincingly and realistically. Nowadays I consider observing body language to be part of my 'homework', but it is also part of a broader fascination with the vagaries of human nature and expression. I often find myself simply watching the people around me – groups of people socialising, an office worker in a hurry for a bus, a teenager acting cool in front of his mates – just observing human behaviour.

Why is body language so important?

Communication comes in many forms, including words, sounds, tone of voice, gestures and touch. The raising of an eyebrow, for instance, can hold a multitude of meanings: disbelief, quizzical uncertainty, interest or disapproval.[6] A sideways glance can indicate mendacity, an attempt to enjoin someone in a joke, or to indicate something unusual.[7] The simple action of tapping a finger can signify irritation, concentrated thinking, impatience or even just the act of counting or tapping out a rhythm.[8]

While we all use and understand a wide range of body language on an instinctive level, we are rarely consciously aware of the messages that our own and other people's bodies are communicating. Developing such a conscious awareness – of even a few of the most basic gestures in body language – can open up a whole new dimension of human behaviour. You can begin to discover what people really mean and whether their intentions are honourable and truthful. You can learn to discern whether your gut instinct about a person is correct and understand how what they are saying is supported by their body language or conflicting with it.

Arming yourself with a knowledge of even a small repertoire of body language gestures can help you to be more effective in all areas of your life. These gestures can help you to communicate better, enhance your popularity with friends and colleagues, and possibly expand your life in ways you may have been too fearful to venture into previously. In the knowledge that we are all human and that we all choose to present a particular image to the outside world, you may no longer be intimidated by people who previously cowed you, and you will have the potential to turn uncomfortable situations into exciting opportunities. An understanding of body language can also make you a more sensitive and compassionate person to be around, in turn enhancing the quality of your life.

6

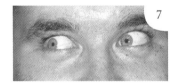
7

8

9

9

Reading body language

Take a seat at any pavement café, order your cappuccino, sit back and watch the dance of life being performed all around you. Imagine that you see a pair of lovers walking by, holding hands and stopping to kiss passionately, totally oblivious to everyone and everything around them. You may think it's obvious what's on their minds: they are lovers and would rather be in bed together than walking down the street.[9] However, to refine your understanding of body language, take a few moments to look at them closely and work out why you have come to that conclusion. They are gazing intently into each other's eyes, oblivious of the world around them.[10] They kiss long and passionately, barely coming up for breath. Notice, too, how close to one another their bodies are. Now take a look at their hands: they are touching each other in private intimate places, caressing one another's face and hair.[11] She is touching the small of his back, and he has his hands firmly on her bottom and is pulling her even closer towards him. Each is physically totally enmeshed with the other.

12

10

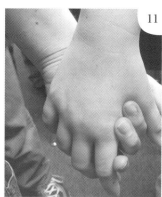
11

Now imagine that a frustrated mother is passing by the café, trying to control an unruly child and struggling with her shopping as she attempts to negotiate a busy high street. Or perhaps you've seen a similar scenario in a shop or a car park.[12] Again, it may take you a fleeting second to come to the conclusion that she is frustrated, over-tired, under-funded and about to give the child a serious chastisement. But how do you know these things? Observe how her whole body is sagging under the weight of her shopping as she struggles to keep pace with her unruly child. She looks as if she is carrying the weight of the world on her shoulders. Her hands are tightly gripping her bags and her knuckles are almost white. Her jaw is set firm, and she shouts at her child through clenched teeth. She puts down her shopping, shakes her head and closes her eyes for a few seconds as though wanting to escape from reality; then, after taking a deep breath, she collects her thoughts, her shopping and her child, and resumes her journey.

13

So how can this information be of any use to you? Well, once you become aware of what particular gestures signify, you can begin to read what people really mean. Whereas it is relatively easy to lie with words, it is much harder – even impossible – to do so with body language. Gestures and actions often belie the message overtly conveyed by the spoken word. For instance, a person who sounds confident and is verbally overpowering in conversation may show themselves to be nervous and defensive if you examine their body language. By making this observation, you can relate to them in a more appropriate way, enabling them to feel more comfortable and possibly to lower their defences. As a result you may notice a physical change in their body language.

14

Let's say you are at an office gathering. If you are aware of some basic body language signals, you need only use a little astute observation to discover who is trying to impress whom, who is making no impression at all, and who is just trying *too* hard.[13] You may notice that one colleague is absorbed in the conversation of an attractive workmate without actually having the slightest interest in what he is talking about![14] You'll be able to see whether the speaker is aware of her colleague's distraction and whether she is responding to the sexual attention or blocking it. Elsewhere in the room, you'll be able to discover who is manipulating the conversation and who is telling downright lies. If one of your colleagues is feeling superior to everyone else, you'll be able to discern this, as well as the resulting friction.

15

Paying a little extra attention to how people gesture towards you during conversations can provide you with heaps of information. You can tell just by the way they are sitting or standing if they are interested in what you have to say, if they agree or disagree with you, if they would rather be elsewhere.[15] You can even tell if they are sexually attracted to you. All of this, without a word being spoken.

16

Being able to assess body language can also help you to avert potentially tense and awkward situations. If you can see that someone is feeling shy and unsure of themselves, you will be able to put them at their ease. If you can see that someone is lying, you can challenge them or avoid being taken in by them. You can learn to recognise real attention from feigned.[16] Even if your judgement and ability to assess a situation are already very astute, knowledge of body language will enhance those skills, giving you an extra edge of confidence and assurance.

Using body language

Communicating through use of body language is natural and instinctive to us. However, by learning the finer points of body language and becoming conscious of how you yourself use them, you can open up for yourself a whole new world of communication.

17

Pay attention to your own body language. What sort of body language do you use when you are happy, excited, sad or depressed? When you feel determined?[17] And when you are agitated and angry? With some practice you can become aware of how you hold yourself as you walk into a room full of strangers, how you stand when you are with a group of colleagues and how your posture changes when someone you love enters a room. It is even possible to observe your body language when you are in the middle of an argument. You may discover hidden feelings and motives that you didn't realise you had.

With just a little practice and a genuine interest, it is possible to make conscious changes to your body language – to choose how you see your world and how you interact within it. Making a habit of using positive body language yourself can, in turn, create huge beneficial changes in your life. You may find that people begin to like and appreciate you more, and even those who usually ignore you may begin to give you recognition. All in all, offering positive gestures to others can open up your life in all sorts of ways.

Imagine, for instance, that you are in a meeting with somebody important and you are feeling nervous and insecure. Because you are afraid, you may avoid making eye contact. You may give this person a very limp handshake and in general use unassertive body language, thus creating a poor impression of yourself. However, if you are familiar with and able to put into practice some learned gestures that communicate confidence, you will alter their perception of you and will in turn feel much better about yourself, so creating a virtuous circle.

Choosing to use appropriate body language is not being false or manipulative. It is simply knowing how you want others to perceive you and conducting yourself accordingly by using supportive body gestures. Good, strong, positive body language simply enables you to feel confident and show the best of yourself.[18]

Using this book

In this book I will not be covering the most basic of body language, as we all know without any technical information that a smile means someone is feeling happy, a nod is a gesture of agreement and a handshake is a sign of greeting.[19] Here I will be concentrating on subtler aspects of body language, the significance of which you may not have considered before.

My aim in this book is not to give you too much indigestible theory but to show you how body language works in real situations. I have therefore highlighted a range of common life situations in which some knowledge of body language is helpful. Human beings are highly evolved animals, and social interaction is instrumental to our continued success on this planet. Understanding more about how we express ourselves can help us to fine-tune our communication skills, which in turn can improve our self-confidence and change the way we are perceived by others. At the same time, when we accurately read what others are thinking and feeling, we can be more sensitive to their needs. An understanding of body language can thus lead to more fruitful and fulfilling relationships, and to a more harmonious and happier life.

20

Chapter 1:
The Basics of Body Language
In Chapter 1, we will be looking at the basic components of body language. We will consider cultural and gender differences, and discuss the body language of children. We will also be considering the fact that gestures and actions are generally made in clusters, within which several components may appear to be inconsistent in meaning. It is therefore important to look at the overall situation and context before drawing firm conclusions from isolated elements of body language.

Chapter 2: Body Language in More Detail
Chapter 2 looks at the specifics of body language in greater depth, starting with the language of the head and working right down to the language of the feet.[20]

Chapter 3: Get Out of My Space

21

In Chapter 3, we will consider the importance of personal space and will see how we use body language to delimit our own body space zones. We will also look at territorial behaviour; meeting, greeting and parting; and how we use body language to make an impression.

Chapter 4: I Know What I Want
Chapter 4 is concerned with how power, confidence and self-assertiveness are expressed in body language. We will be looking at how you can use the body language of power to get what you want, and will also be considering how status is related to body language.

Chapter 5: I Want to Make an Impression
In Chapter 5 we will be considering the kind of body language to use in order to impress employers, colleagues and friends. We will be looking at how you can best present yourself in situations such as interviews, networking events and social occasions.[21]

Chapter 6: Do You Fancy Me?

In Chapter 6 we look at flirting and sexual attraction. Actions and gestures give tell-tale signs that a person fancies us. Being aware of some of them can save us considerable embarrassment and angst – feelings that we will all have experienced at some time.[22]

Chapter 7: I Care About You

From sexual attraction we move to caring and offering support. In Chapter 7 we will be exploring the body language we use to comfort and reassure others. We will also be looking at helpful ways to communicate non-verbally in an emergency – a skill that once mastered can even save lives.

Chapter 8: Are You Listening to Me?

Chapter 8 looks at paying attention – or not. It will show you how to indicate that you are listening and how to tell if people are listening to you.

Chapter 9: Who's Stressed Out?

In Chapter 9 we consider some of the many physical signs that tell us a person is under stress. Being able to spot these signs in ourselves and other people can help us to deal more effectively with everyday situations.[23]

Chapter 10: So Who's Lying?

Chapter 10 addresses one of my favourite areas of body language, and one that warrants a book in its own right. In this chapter we will be discovering how to tell if a person is lying, be it a white lie or a complicated piece of deception. Being lied to can be infuriating and hurtful, but watching another person's discomfort as they attempt to tell a lie can be a highly amusing pastime – take it from me!

Chapter 11: You and Whose Army?

Chapter 11 deals with the body language of aggression and insult. We live in a world of high tension, and the ability to spot signals of potential aggression can be helpful in defusing potentially serious situations. At the same time, a knowledge of our own body language can help us to avoid giving aggressive responses ourselves.

24

Chapter 12: Do As I Do – and As I Say

Finally, Chapter 12 briefly considers mixed messages – those moments when our words are saying one thing but our body language is telling a completely different story. This can lead to mistrust, confusion and the breakdown of communication.

A general understanding of body language can help us to communicate more effectively in all areas of our lives, while observing our own body language can highlight many interesting behavioural traits. The results can be enlightening, empowering and often amusing. Most important of all, raising our awareness of body language can help us to bring about positive dynamic changes in our lives.[24] The exercises included in each chapter of this book have been carefully chosen to help you in this fascinating journey of self-discovery.

1 The Basics of Body Language

To a greater or lesser degree, all animals on the planet have learned to communicate with each other by using some combination of signals, gestures and sounds.[1] In the case of our own species, our uniquely developed brain has, over time, allowed us to develop advanced verbal communication. This does not mean, however, that we have lost any of the older body language that evolved among our earliest primate ancestors.[2] Although we use it in a largely subconscious way, our body language remains of central importance to our expression of needs, feelings, opinions and intentions. Indeed, we use body language as our primary means of communication just like every other animal. Because of the sophistication of our verbal skills and the priority we give to speech in our daily dealings with others, we tend to forget that the spoken word forms only a small fraction of our communication. Recent scientific studies suggest that body language accounts for up to 65 per cent of interactive communication. Tone of voice accounts for around 30 per cent, and – remarkably – the spoken word accounts for only about 5 per cent of our communication.

1

2

Our facial expressions, gestures and postures are fundamental aspects of human behaviour. While cultural differences do influence our body language to a degree, much of it is universal. Wherever in the world we happen to find ourselves, we can instantly recognise a welcoming smile as a gesture of friendship.[3] Similarly, we are in little doubt that a clenched fist shaken in our faces is an aggressive or hostile gesture.[4]

3

We learn this language from the moment of our entry into the world, in our mother's arms. Gradually our understanding of it grows until we are able to interpret and use a wide range of touches, gestures, movements and expressions. While we may have developed such technological innovations as the telephone, fax and email to exploit our ability to use speech and its written form, body language will always be the fundamental and clearest form of human communication.

4

5

What is body language?

The term 'body language' designates the vast array of physical movements that occur both consciously and unconsciously all over our body as we communicate. These may be subtle movements of the eyes, shifts in our posture, facial expressions, gestures with codified meanings (such as a shake of the head for 'no', a beckoning gesture for 'come here'), or holding hands to say 'I love you'.[5] For the most part, we go about our routine activities oblivious to the fact that we are constantly sending, receiving and processing these signals, and that this communication is also picked up and understood by those around us.

Body language is made up of a number of different sub-groups. These are outlined below.

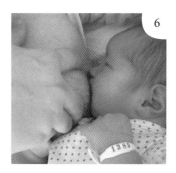

6

Actions

In the process of communication we perform an almost infinite number of actions. These can be divided into several different categories.

Genetic

These actions are instilled in our genetic make-up, and are part of our basic survival equipment. For example, we know instinctively how to suckle as babies.[6] We also know how to cry when we are hungry or in need of attention.[7] When we get older, we cry spontaneously when we are upset, just as we laugh spontaneously in response to something funny.

7

Environmental

We learn these actions from the environment around us as we develop. For instance, we naturally mimic others in our peer group. Just as children and teenagers often adopt a particular vocabulary in order to appear 'cool' and to be accepted among their friends, they may also alter the way they walk and the gestures they make.

Cultural

Closely related to our environment is our culture. Some of our actions are the result of belonging to a distinct community, sect, group or even sports team that has developed certain unique body language habits. For example, the New Zealand All Blacks rugby team ritually perform the haka, a Maori war dance before each game they play.[8] The gestures formalised in the dance derive from the ancient Maori body language of challenge and confrontation. Even a simple thing like a gesture of greeting may have its roots in our culture. While in the West we often shake hands on meeting, in India people bring their hands together and bow their heads.[9]

Physiological

Certain of our actions are purely physiological responses, reflex actions over which we have virtually no control. For instance, if someone raises their fist to you, you may involuntarily flinch – a gesture of fear and submission.[10] Of particular interest to us here are the involuntary reflex dilations of the pupil, a very reliable form of body language, primarily because they cannot be consciously controlled.[11]

Professional

Certain professions carry with them their own specific patterns of body language. A chauffeur, for example, is expected to behave in a reserved and deferential manner, making minimal eye contact and keeping his or her actions unobtrusive and subservient. Whereas it would be considered appropriate for a chauffeur to open the car door for a passenger, it would be considered totally inappropriate for him or her to wind the window down nonchalantly and have a cigarette while ignoring their employer.

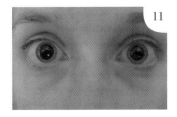

12

Postures

Postures are the various stances our bodies assume when we are resting, relaxing, waiting, in conversation or in some other semi-static position. These can be surprisingly varied. Imagine, for example, the different postures that might be displayed by a bouncer on duty at the door of a nightclub, a hotel porter, a mother meeting her child at the school gates, an expectant father nervously waiting for a baby to be born, an office receptionist, a police officer, a chauffeur.[12] Each body posture will reflect the occupation and/or emotional situation of the person, and will be influenced by a combination of factors, such as social status, current energy level, training (for example, a ballet dancer is unlikely to slouch) and the demands that are regularly made on the body. For instance, a hairdresser, whose work involves bending over clients all day, may be round-shouldered.[13]

Gestures

A gesture is a visual signal in the form of a physical action, and is made either consciously (as in waving to a friend) or unconsciously (as in scratching your nose). When we are alone, we tend to be mostly unaware of our gestures, and they may be few in number. Once we are in company, however, our consciousness of gesture is heightened, and we tend to extend our gestural range in response to others in the environment around us. Notice, for example, what happens when a stunningly attractive woman enters a room full of men. Not only will the men shift their body posture, standing upright and holding in their stomachs, but they will also exchange glances and tiny gestures with each other, acknowledging among themselves what they are seeing and feeling

13

about her. Conversely, when a woman finds herself approaching a group of attractive men, she may slow her step and swing her hips in order to exaggerate the attractiveness of her figure.

Expressions

Human beings display by far the widest and most subtle range of facial expressions in the animal kingdom, a vast repertoire that has evolved as a result of the highly social and communication-oriented nature of our species. It is therefore not surprising to learn that we also have the largest number of facial muscles. In fact, we gesture more with our faces than with any other part of our bodies. Just consider, for instance, the myriad of meanings that a slight upturn of the eyebrow can have, depending on the situation and the other body language and verbal communication it is combined with. As human beings, we are fine-tuned to notice the slightest of facial movements, even if we cannot fully interpret them. It is fair to say that the eyes and mouth are our most expressive features.

14

The eyes are said to be the window of the soul, while the enigmatic smile of the Mona Lisa has captivated us for hundreds of years, making this portrait the most visited painting of all time.[14]

Signs and signals

We make many signs and signals without any conscious knowledge. Some of these may be extremely subtle, such as raising an eyebrow when confronted with a deception or suppressing a yawn during an important conversation. As our moods change, we make unconscious pupil signals – our pupils dilate when we are excited and contract when our feelings are negative. Other signals, such as pointing and directing, are overt and expressive, and some signs can even be vulgar or offensive. When we are trying to suppress our true feelings, we consciously resist making any signals whatsoever. On the other hand, we may use exaggerated signals in certain situations, for example when someone tells us a joke that is not funny but which we feel we must laugh at for the sake of politeness.

15

International and cultural aspects

Much body language – such as a smile and open arms, or a clenched fist – can be understood instantly anywhere in the world. However, some body language of the non-genetic and non-physiological kind is national or regional. The differences may be subtle or they may be marked. Some gestures that have completely innocuous meanings in one culture are offensive in another. For instance, the Western world's 'okay buddy' sign is in some Eastern societies a defamatory gesture referring to the anal anatomy. In Malta this gesture is an insulting way of indicating that a person is gay, and it is also regarded as offensive in Greece.[15]

If you are travelling abroad, it is wise to consult a book about the region you are visiting so that you can reduce the possibility of unintentionally causing offence or, equally, of making a fool of yourself! Many travel books make a point of explaining any distinctive local gestures and signs. However, such warnings should not put you off trying to communicate. While some gestures are peculiar to particular cultures or communities, there are also many that are commonly used and universally understood all over the world. In a country where we do not speak the language we can usually manage to give and receive basic information such as names and directions quite effectively, if somewhat crudely, by using body language. Finding somewhere to eat, getting simple directions and bartering for goods can be achieved with enthusiastic nodding and shaking of heads, flailing of arms and strong handshakes.[16] A beaming smile is recognised anywhere.[17]

Gender and body language

It is commonly accepted that there are differences between the genders, whether these are genetic or cultural (or a bit of both) in basis. Similarly, some aspects of body language are, either by nature or nurture, gender-specific.

16

17

These days the trend is away from maintaining rigid gender differences. The practice of dressing baby girls uniformly in pink and boys in blue is no longer quite as general as it once was, and the fashion has moved further towards non-gender-specific names such as Charlie, Alex, Bailey and Cameron. Perhaps this fashion is merely that; however, my own feeling is that it indicates a new and more flexible social attitude towards gender.

Nevertheless, some gender differences continue to flourish, as I discovered when I spent some time working in Theatre in Education. Part of this work was observational research with young adults. We invited a small group of young girls to meet together for the first time, allocating them 30 minutes to get to know one another. The girls very quickly introduced themselves and began to talk. They moved closer towards each other, exchanged personal details, listened to each other and had begun to establish friendships within the first few minutes.[18] By the end of the 30-minute session, these 'strangers' were huddled together chatting away like good friends. Some friendly hands-on body contact had been made, such as arm touching.[19]

Next we invited a small group of boys to meet together for the first time, again allocating them 30 minutes to get acquainted. The difference from the girls' group was marked. The boys maintained a wide physical distance between one another, were hesitant to make contact and resisted small talk. Once a common theme was found, such as football, the conversation centred on the subject matter. No personal information was exchanged and no physical contact was made.[20]

Later in life, these general observations still seem to be significantly true of the genders. A group of women will sit closely together, making friendly body contact such as arm- and hand-touching, and engaging in conversation that is personal and intimate in nature. Men, on the other hand, will stay further apart from each other, will avoid touching and will engage in more information-based conversation, feeling at greater ease displaying emotions in connection with subjects such as sport or work.

21

Female body language

The physical differences between the sexes dictate certain differences in body language. Women's bodies are naturally geared towards childbearing, regardless of the vagaries of fashion. Compared with men, we have larger hips, fuller breasts, narrower waists and tend to be shorter and lighter, with more body fat and less muscle. While many women desperately attempt to attain the currently fashionable waif-like, hip-less figure, paradoxically, the average female figure is changing shape in the opposite direction. Statistics show that the average female waist is becoming thicker and that women are increasing in both weight and height.

Meanwhile, some younger women are attempting to bridge the gender gap by developing what are traditionally considered to be more masculine traits. These trendy young 'laddettes' are boisterous, outspoken and ready to down a pint with the next guy.

Gait and posture

The nature of the female skeleton and musculature dictates a gait that is different from a man's. Women typically walk with a swaying motion, buttocks and hips moving from side to side. Our stride is also relatively short.[21] Another typical aspect of female body posture is that, due to our narrow shoulders, we tend to hold our arms closer to our body than a man does.[22] This trait is sometimes mimicked by gay men.

22

Sexuality and attraction

When relaxed and in the company of men, a woman will instinctively sit with her legs slightly wider apart than she would otherwise or draw attention to her genital area by a strategically placed hand. When walking past a man or a group of men, she will hold herself upright, push out her breasts, hold in her stomach and roll her hips in a swaying motion, drawing attention to her childbearing hips and her femininity. This body language is subconsciously driven and is adopted in response to men even by women (for example lesbians) who have no actual sexual interest in the men around them.

When a woman is relishing her sexuality, she may become obsessed with her hair, using it to draw attention to herself – especially when she is receiving admiring glances. The next time you have an opportunity, just stop and observe – we pay an extraordinary amount of attention to our hair. We play with it, twiddling the ends and twisting it round our fingers.[23] We flick it over our shoulders, pull it over our eyes and then toss it out of the way.[24] The fascination is apparently endless – regardless of whether the hair is long or short.[25]

23

When a woman wants to signify seductive intent to a specific person, she will frequently lower her eyes, slowly flutter her eyelashes and give a sideways peek-a-boo glance at the object of her desire. (This signal is also used by gay men as a sexual come-on.)

You may be thinking that these gestures are both crude and out of date; surely in this day and age we strong independent women do not do these things? But we do, and what's more we can't help it! We may do it in a more subtle or discreet way than the above descriptions suggest, but we certainly do it. Make a point of observing other women's behaviour in the presence of an attractive potential partner and you will soon see for yourself. When someone takes our fancy, the Neanderthal can appear in us all, no matter how hard we try to suppress her!

24

Defensiveness

If a woman is feeling defensive, she will tend to sit with her legs crossed and directed away from the action. If she is feeling extremely defensive she will (if physically able to do so) wrap one leg around the other, clearly signalling that all the shutters are down. It is interesting to note that this leg position has not been observed being used by men – in any culture.

25

Eyes, mouth and make-up

To enhance our attractiveness, we women spend millions of pounds each year on make-up and cosmetics. Throughout history we have always sought to enhance and exaggerate our facial features. The traditional Geisha girls of Japan whiten their faces and paint their features back in again. In the theatre, heavy eye make-up has always been used to draw the audience's attention to this focal point of the face that conveys so much emotion. The Ancient Egyptians were renowned for their use of kohl, which they applied to accentuate the allure of their eyes.[26]

If I was ever invited to be a guest on the radio programme *Desert Island Discs*, when the presenter asked me which one item I would like to take with me, it would without doubt be my lipstick, which is my personal obsession and an item I take everywhere with me. Why is lipstick so important to me and many other women? For myself, I would say it is because when I am

26

wearing lipstick I feel dressed and complete. However, according to the renowned anthropologist Desmond Morris, we use lipstick to draw attention to our lips because they symbolise female genitalia. Our primate ancestors walked on all fours and had their genitalia constantly on display, as does our close relative the chimpanzee. When a female ape is sexually interested and available for intercourse, her genitalia become reddened and enlarged, thus giving a clear signal to the male of her willingness. Although this biological reaction is still a part of female human sexual arousal, our social behaviour has changed just a bit – thank goodness! Nowadays it is just our faces that are on show, so we smile, tilt our heads and flutter our eyelashes.[27] But our basic primate urge is still so strong that, according to Morris, we also redden and moisten our lips to resemble our vulva and give out a subliminal 'come on' message.

27

Of course, none of this information goes through most of our minds when we put lipstick on; like me, most women probably feel that they simply look better wearing it.[28] However, it does explain the prevalence of open-mouthed, wet-lipped female images on the front covers of men's magazines: with their promise of sexual gratification, they sell more copies.[29]

29

28

Male body language

As we have already noted, men are generally taller than women. They have narrower hips, broader chests, more muscle mass and less body fat. In our primeval days, men were the hunters. They travelled long distances in search of game, while the women tended to stay in one place to gather fruit, vegetables and grains, and to bring up the children and care for the old and infirm. Men's bodies have evolved for speed and strength, and the physical structure of the male body determines its posture and movement.[30] Men generally have a longer stride than women, and their broad chests and muscular shoulders ensure that their arms are held away from their torso.

Machismo

The typical macho male image that can be seen all over glossy magazines is that of a muscular, often bare-chested, male with his legs straddled and his feet placed firmly and squarely apart.[31] He is proudly exposing his crotch area, thus displaying his manhood to potential sexual partners, and his broad open chest is his sign of bravery and self-assertion. Standing with legs firmly planted apart is also a signal of courage and bravado to other men, as this stance exposes the vulnerable genitalia without fear. (The genitalia are the body part a man will automatically protect first; this is often observable when men are playing football.)

An aggressive version of this macho stance, which has often been depicted in westerns, is the 'thumbs-in-belt' pose. The thumbs tucked into the belt thrust forward and draw attention to the exposed genitalia, proudly affirming lack of fear. This posture has recently been adopted by some women, especially in the pop music industry, and can been seen on several album covers. The woman often wears a bra top and cut-off jeans, and has her hands in her belt and her thumbs on display. The combination of male stance and female eroticism signifies not only an attitude of dominance but also sexual control over men. (For more information see page 36.)

Standing with hands placed firmly on hips is also a masculine display of authority, assertiveness and possible confrontation. Gay men often put their hands on their hips in an effeminate way, which does not have the same overtly aggressive intensity, although it may sometimes be a gesture of passive aggression.

Children's body language

In London a new body language workshop has recently been created for parents of pre-school-age children. By being able to interpret the non-verbal gestures of their babies and young children, it has been shown that carers are better able to understand their babies' needs.

The body language of a child is open, truthful and a wonderful place to begin your observation of non-verbal communication, being free and spontaneous and easy to read. Even before they have begun to talk, children have an impressive array of gestures, facial expressions and stances at their disposal. There's little doubt that the puckered face, tears and rigid posture in the photograph indicate distress.[34]

Even very young babies are observed to shake their heads from side to side when they have taken enough food. It is thought that the universal gesture of shaking the head side to side to indicate 'no' comes from this instinctive signal of refusal.[32] (In Asia, the shaking of the head has come to mean 'I do not know' or 'maybe'; however, this gesture is not innate but has evolved out of a culture of extreme politeness, in which it is considered undesirable to offend another by saying 'no' outright.)

32

Have you ever attempted to negotiate the supermarket while dealing with a crying, screaming child? Their body is tense, their fists are clenched, their facial muscles are contorted with rage and tears are pouring from their eyes. Whatever you do to calm the child down only seems to have the opposite effect. Until, that is, the magic moment when you give them the packet of sweets they have been screaming for and the racket abruptly stops.[33]

33

34

Within moments the body language of the child has miraculously changed. Gone are the tears; their face has lit up; they are smiling and maybe even chuckling with delight: body language in its purest form.

35

By the age of about eight or nine years, children have evolved a complex and free-flowing repertoire of body language which is easy to read. Happiness and sadness, anger and aggression are all clearly visible.[35] When telling a lie, for example, a child will often raise one or both hands to cover his or her mouth, as if in an attempt to stop the words coming out.[36] Later in life this gesture becomes more refined, until in adulthood we might need a trained eye to detect it. It could, for instance, be passed off as scratching the nose. We will explore the fascinating topic of lies in Chapter 10.

Single and combination gestures

In this section of the book, we will start by looking at a few common arm and leg gestures in isolation and will move on to consider some of them in combination.

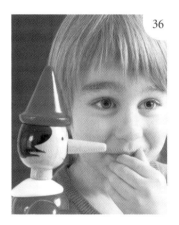
36

Single gestures

The following basic arm and leg gestures are commonly used and easy to familiarise yourself with. Watch and take note of when, where and why people use them and – more importantly – when, where and why you make them yourself.

Folded arms

Folded or partially folded arms function as a defensive barrier, creating a distance between us and someone else. They may indicate a need to protect and comfort ourselves, or they may signify that we disagree with what someone is saying.[37] We often use this gesture when we are meeting someone for the first time. As we begin to feel more comfortable in their company, we generally relax our arms. (For more information on folded arms see pages 86–7.)

37

38

Crossed legs

Crossed legs are another form of barrier that is often used in conjunction with folded arms and clearly shows a person who is behaving defensively for some reason.[38] The legs are generally held away from the 'attacker'. In a standing position, one ankle crossed in front of another is a similar defensive gesture.

Be aware, however, that people frequently cross their legs (or ankles) simply in order to make themselves more comfortable.[39] When you catch yourself crossing your own legs, notice whether you are doing so in response to a negative message or just to shift to a more comfortable position. (For more on crossed legs see pages 87–8.)

39

Foot positions

The position of a person's feet can tell you to whom or what their attention is drawn, for the feet will generally be pointing to the person or object of interest.[40]

Combination gestures

When you first begin to study body language, you will discover two frustrating things. One is that no one keeps still long enough for you to scrutinise their every gesture. The other is that neither do they generally make one gesture in isolation. As we flit rapidly from one thought or feeling to another, our body language changes instantaneously in order to reflect each one.

40

We tend to make several gestures in quick succession, some of which may well contradict one another (since we often experience contradictory thoughts and emotions almost simultaneously). The best advice I can give when you are first delving into the fascinating world of body language is to become familiar with a few basic gestures and take note only of these.

Another helpful hint is to consider the overall situation or conversation and beware of jumping to a conclusion too quickly on the basis of an isolated gesture, as your conclusion may be incorrect. A person sitting with arms and legs folded and their head pointing downwards may not be feeling negative and defensive but may have a bad stomach ache.

Consider the cross-legged position. To be sure whether it is really being adopted defensively, you will need to observe whether it is for comfort, in the first place – such as someone playing an instrument – or if any other negative gestures are being used. For instance, if the person is also leaning backwards, this is a sure sign that they would like to create a distance between themselves and the person they are talking to. Likewise with folded arms.[41] If a person is also actively avoiding eye contact, it is safe to conclude that they are in a negative frame of mind. If they then state verbally that they agree with the person they are talking to, you will know that what they are saying and thinking are not the same!

Let's look at a familiar situation and consider the range of body language that might be clearly visible in it. Imagine that you and a friend are sitting in a café having a chat.[42] You notice that your friend has her legs crossed and that her feet are pointing towards you, the foot position showing clearly that she is interested in what you have to say. There is a considerable amount of mirror imaging going on. For example, you both pick up your cups at the same time and smile at the same time, again indicating that you are getting along fine. Then you say something that seems innocuous enough to you and, apparently totally out of the blue, your friend changes her body language. She sits back, crosses her legs away from you and folds her arms.

41

42

43

44

You realise that for some reason she has put up her defences. Whatever you said did not go down well. Had she changed her body posture in a casual way, then she might have been finding a more comfortable position, but in this instance it was done quickly and just at the point that you made your remark. What you said has clearly made a difference to her mood.

Just then a man you do not know very well but would very much like to walks past your table. The conversation pauses as you follow him with your eyes, offer a smile and without thinking change your posture. You sit upright, adjust your clothes for reassurance, give another smile and then turn back round to face your friend, who is fully aware that your attention has been attracted elsewhere. You give a nervous cough, clear your throat and smile at your friend as you make an attempt to pick up the conversation. However, your friend has now not only put her defences up but is also taking what appears to be her last mouthful of coffee. She slams down her cup and gives you a cold stare.[43] Then she checks the messages on her mobile, severing eye contact. Both of you have now lost track of the conversation. She shuffles around in her seat, making a movement to leave. Contrast that with the relaxed, forward-leaning posture of two friends sharing a coffee break.[44]

In a very small space of time there have been many gestures, actions and expressions, all of which are totally natural and commonplace in everyday life. Though in such a situation we generally understand perfectly well on a subliminal level what all this body language means, it is unlikely that we are consciously aware of it, and certainly not of the amount of non-verbal signals we have actually given and received. When you first begin to delve into the real-time reading of body language, you may well be overwhelmed by the vast array of gestures that we use in any interchange.

Considering context

Before jumping to conclusions about a person's body language, it is wise to take into consideration everything you know about the overall situation. Let's consider that you are in a meeting and someone is giving you several signs of negativity. Their legs are crossed against you, their arms are folded defensively, they are not looking you in the eye and they are leaning slightly backwards – yet verbally they are agreeing with you.[45] Now imagine that you know this person has just had a volatile argument with their partner. This information changes the scenario completely, since it is likely that they are preoccupied with thoughts about the argument and cannot disassociate from them. They are distressed, upset and angry, but not with you. They may well agree with what you are saying but cannot focus on the conversation.

Now let's imagine that you are with your elderly mother, who is not used to travelling and socialising. For a treat you are taking her to the opera and are having pre-theatre drinks at the Savoy. The people around you are elegant and refined. Your mother is sitting with her legs crossed and her arms folded, but not because she is angry or in disagreement with you. She is simply out of her depth and intimidated by her surroundings, and would much rather be at home having a cup of tea and watching television with her slippers on. Her negative body language relates to the uncomfortable situation she finds herself in.

So remember, if you are going to make accurate interpretations of body language, you must always consider the overall situation and the character of the person concerned as well as all the

individual gestures, postures and expressions. Don't jump to conclusions too quickly based on just one element in a complex, multi-layered picture. For example, let's look in turn at the five people in the photograph.[46] For convenience, let's label them from the left: Number one, and so on.

Number one is slightly slumped in her chair and looking vaguely distracted; she could be bored. But look at the way she is clasping her hands and the awkward position of her feet, which looks more like anxiety. Now bring context into the equation. If she were sitting at the side of a school reunion she didn't want to attend, then stultifying boredom would be your conclusion. But she is clearly waiting for a job interview and feeling anxious that it's not going to go well and that she doesn't have what it takes to get the job.

Number two has an open posture with a straight back and a broad smile. There's not much doubt he's feeling fairly pleased with himself and quite relaxed and confident. But is there a hint of falsehood in that smile? Does he just want to persuade his old classmates that he's doing really well – or hope he can use his charm in the interview when he doesn't quite have the right qualifications? You'd need to observe more closely to draw your conclusions.

Number three is sitting confidently upright – the class swot? The most business-like candidate? Now look at the clasped hands, defensively crossed ankles and anxious biting of her lips. She is uncomfortable with her surroundings – whether a get-together or an interview – and is putting up barriers to anyone else in the room.

Number four is perhaps more straightforward. She looks quite relaxed in her posture, sitting comfortably and neither bolt upright nor slumped down. She looks quietly confident, whatever the circumstances, and her crossed legs look more like a comfort gesture than a defensive one. Although she is looking at her watch, which could be interpreted as a sign of impatience, it's more likely she simply wants to know the time!

At first glance, Number five has an open, not a defensive, posture. However, he is biting his thumb and, most importantly, is turning away from the other people in the room, distancing himself from them. We can infer that he doesn't have much in common with them and is anxious to keep himself to himself.

Remember, then, that is a fascinating study that offers opportunities to learn more every day, so always keep your eye on the bigger picture and be careful not to judge too quickly.

2 Body Language in More Detail

In this chapter we will be taking a closer look at body language. We will be starting with the way we stand and will then be going on a journey around the body, considering the body language of the different parts from top to toe.

What's your standing?

The way we hold ourselves gives the onlooker a great deal of information. The following are some examples:

1

- Confident person: stands erect[1]
- Proud person: holds their head up high[2]
- Sad and dejected person: shrinks themselves in to appear smaller than they are
- Person with the weight of the world upon their shoulders: has rounded shoulders and stoops, so that you can almost see the burden they are carrying[3]
- Fraught and uptight person: cannot stand still (as their agitated thoughts transmit themselves to their body)
- Irritated person: may scratch themselves (indicating that the irritation has 'got under their skin')

2

3

4

5

6

- Enthusiastic person: finds it difficult to stand still (their energy is saying, 'Let's get on with it')
- Aggressive person: has both hands firmly planted on the hips

Cast your mind back to Del Boy in the TV series *Only Fools and Horses* as he prepares himself for a confrontation.[4] He demonstrates a typical aggressive and ready-for-action stance. He opens up his coat, placing his fists on his hips, juts out his chin and says: 'I'm going to have a word with him!' By opening his coat he is exposing his chest and heart, showing lack of fear and readiness for a challenge. Placing his fist on his hips makes him appear broader than he actually is, just as in the animal world the puffed-out wings of a goose exaggerate its size in order to intimidate its opponent.

Another much used aggressive stance was demonstrated by the Duke, John Wayne. With his feet planted firmly apart and his thumbs looped into his trouser belt, he assumed the stereotypical cowboy pose to intimidate his opponent – who would take one look at the great man and scurry away.[5]

In more recent times, this pose has been adopted and adapted by women wishing to look assertive. Madonna, for instance, at one time took up the sexually assertive cowgirl look. Similarly, pop star Christina Aguilera can be seen on her *Stripped* album cover wearing a sexually exposing bikini top and cut-off denim shorts, with her thumbs tucked into her shorts waist.[6] Her body language is displaying a sexually assertive and potentially aggressive image. Of course, on an album cover a person's stance reflects their image and marketing – the way they want to be seen rather than the way they necessarily are. At one time or another in our lives most of us will want to project an image that is at odds with the way we are actually feeling.

7

Imagine, for example, that you are after a top job. You will probably power-dress for the interview and try to speak with confidence and authority, and yet you may be quaking inside. If you do not use the kind of strong positive body language that fits the image, however, you are unlikely to pull the interview off.[7] The way you present yourself to others visually and verbally will not be convincing in any situation unless it is complemented by your body language.

My brother-in-law is an under-cover police officer and is remarkably good at his job, the reason being that he has the ability to blend into the background and lose his policeman's body posture – unlike many of his colleagues. A lot of plain-clothed police officers enter a public place with the intention of being discreet, but – no matter how much effort they have made with their plain clothes – they can be easily spotted. This is because what they are wearing conflicts with the body language they are using. They may be dressed in casual clothes, trying to give a laid-back impression, but their body posture and the way they walk gives them away. They command a position of high status with the full backing of the law and they exude authority. As a result, they generally cannot help walking tall, acting confident and looking people straight in the eye.

The more confident and positive we are feeling, the more upright and open our body posture and stance will be. The reverse is also true. When we are feeling defensive and negative, our body closes in around itself and we tend to barricade ourselves behind folded arms and crossed legs. We may even choose to sit behind a table, thus hiding ourselves away as an extra defence. When we feel depressed, our body seems weighed down by our worries and concerns and appears smaller. We may begin to stoop, as if we cannot fully support ourselves. Good posture is more than something your mum may have nagged you about; it denotes a healthy attitude and a healthy mind.[8]

8

9

10

Exercise: How your mood and energy level affects your posture

Different moods and mental states have different energy levels. This energy manifests itself in the way we stand and move. Violence, aggression and anger, for example, have exceptionally high energy levels, as does fear. To a lesser degree so, too, do competitiveness and confidence. In general, the more negative we are feeling, the lower our energy levels are likely to be. Use this exercise to observe how the different types of energy generated by different moods affect your posture and the way you move.

At various points throughout the day take time to consider your overall mood.

- Notice what your energy levels are like.
- Now observe how mood and energy level are reflected in your body posture. For example, are you feeling positive today, full of energy and zapping around getting everything done with a smile on your face? Are your strides confident and purposeful? Can you look the world in the face? Or are you in a foul mood with nil energy and wanting to hide from the world?
- Consider what is happening to your body. Does it feel heavy and cumbersome? Does it want to slump into a chair?[9] Does it feel upright and tall? Are you relaxed, especially around the neck and shoulders?[10] Or are you tense and stiff?

Armed with your new knowledge of how mood and energy level affect your posture, go out and observe other people. By looking at their posture, see what conclusions you can come to about the way they are feeling and how energised they are.

How near, how far: distance and angles

The closer a person stands to you, the more interested in you they are likely to be. When someone is fascinated by you or what you are saying, they will move in close; whereas if they are not engaged in this way, they will keep their distance. By turning their back on you and looking elsewhere, a person signals a complete lack of interest and perhaps aversion.

Where a person sits and how their body is angled towards yours will clearly communicate how interested they are in you – or in someone else nearby. If they cross their legs so that a knee points in your direction, they are clearly interested in you. However, if their knee is pointing towards someone else, that is where their real interest lies. Toe pointing is another indication of interest, and can be seen more clearly in the standing position. (For more on knee- and toe-pointing see page 134.)

When two people know each other very well and are content just to be together rather than indulge in intense conversation, they will often sit side by side.[11] Face to face is a more intimate seating position. Sitting at angles to another person makes the conversation less intense and opens up the relationship to the outside. Two people sitting at a pavement café, might take this position, in which they can easily make eye contact with each other without restricting their view of what is going on in the street.

In conversation, two people who feel easy and relaxed with each other will often stand at the same angle. This position allows eye contact but does not exclude anyone else from joining them. Two people standing facing each other suggests a private or intimate conversation and tends to keep others out.[12] Where a group of people are standing and talking, the toe-pointing gesture can often be seen, indicating where different individuals' attention is drawn. The angle of people's bodies can likewise show where in the group their interest lies.

11

12

13 Exercise: Distances and angles in body posture

Use this exercise to become aware of how you and others use closeness and distance and body angles to express intimacy with and interest in the different people you spend time with.

- The next time you are in a public place, notice the distances and angles between people gathered together in groups. Observe how people sit or stand when they are engaged in intimate conversation. Are they close to one another? Are they face to face? Take note of toe- or knee-pointing gestures and of body angles.[13]
- The next time you are sitting privately with a loved one, take a moment to become aware of the angle and positioning of your bodies. Are you sitting side by side (a comfortable, relaxed positioning) or are you facing each other and gazing into one another's eyes (a much more intense positioning)?[14]

Heads up: head positions and movements

If you pay close attention to any conversation, you will notice that when we are talking we all make many movements with our heads. At first these may appear random and meaningless; in fact, however, each of these movements plays a role in expressing our true feelings. Each nod, shake or turn of the head clearly communicates a thought or intention.

14

The nod

We use head movements most often during conversation, the nod being the most frequently employed. A nod can be used to say hello and to acknowledge someone else's presence. It indicates 'yes' and also functions as an 'I'm paying attention' gesture as we listen to another person speak. In this case, the nod may not necessarily indicate that the listener agrees with what is being said but may rather be an acknowledgement and an encouragement to the speaker to continue. Women in particular look for and use this encouraging form of nod as a measure of the listener's attention, and may see its absence as rudeness. Whatever the gender concerned, if the listener withholds the nodding gesture consistently, the person talking will cut short whatever they are saying and usually ceases speaking. You may notice that television interviewers use the nod very frequently in order to encourage interviewees to speak fully and at length.

We also use nodding gestures when we speak. A slow nod is used to emphasise something we feel is significant. When we want acknowledgement from a listener, again, we will use a nod, as if to say, 'Do you understand?' [15]

Exercise: Nod or not

Try out this exercise to see for yourself what effect nodding and withholding nodding has on a conversation.

- The next time you are listening to someone talking, nod your head more frequently than usual, while at the same time giving the speaker direct eye contact. This will convey interest to them, and you should notice that they speak for longer, elaborating on their subject. (A word of caution here, however. Make sure you don't nod too much, otherwise you will appear rather foolish, over-enthusiastic and a bit like a puppy waiting for its ball to be thrown!)
- Pick another occasion when someone is talking to you and try withholding nodding gestures. Notice how this interferes with the flow of their speech. The absence of nodding will imply a lack of interest on your part, and they are likely to cut short whatever they are saying.

Lowering of the head

This gesture is used as a sign of respect and humility, and can be seen in places of worship and on solemn occasions.[16] We bow our heads when meeting people we venerate or hold in esteem, such as the Pope or a president, in so doing acknowledging their higher status. We also lower our heads as a mark of respect for the dead and when being confronted about a misdemeanour for which we feel guilt and shame – just as a child hangs its head when being scolded by a parent.

When speaking, we lower our heads as we come to the end of a sentence. We then lift our heads, take a breath and begin the next sentence.

Head to head

Lovers use the head-to-head gesture to express their intimacy, often without uttering any words.[17] This touching gesture also sometimes occurs between two very good friends and is an expression of their closeness.[18] Confidantes use this gesture when discussing private matters in order not to be overhead. Children, too, can often be seen communicating *tête-à-tête* (literally 'head to head') as they plan mischief or share secrets.

A completely different head-to-head gesture is the violent clash of opposing rivals in combat. This may start with people 'facing up' to each other with their faces as close as possible without touching but can escalate to either a full-on banging of heads or one party head-butting the other. This is clearly an aggressive act and is often on display among rival supporters at football matches.

Head on another's shoulder

This gesture is used in the main by women and children to show affection, though gay men may also use it for the same purpose. The head on the shoulder is a sign of endearment, a signal that this person likes you, feels comfortable with you and trusts you.[19] A head on someone's shoulder accompanied by an exhausted sigh is a request for emotional support. I have observed this gesture being used by men with their intimate partners.

The head flick

This gesture is used to point to a person or thing without using the eyes or hands. The head indicates the object of interest. A flick of the head upwards together with upturned eyes is a gesture of exasperation.[20] The downward head flick can also form part of a military greeting and salute – for example, the Nazi salute was made by clicking together the heels and sharply flicking the head downwards.

The double-take

This action is an actor's *pièce de résistance* and takes considerable practice to perform authentically – in the world of British sitcom, David Jason as Del Boy in *Only Fools and Horses* and Ronnie Barker as Fletch in *Porridge* have mastered the double-take to perfection.[21]

A double-take occurs when a person sees something or hears a comment and without initially registering its significance begins to turn their head away; however, in the middle of this action the penny drops and they turn their head back to the scene or person with a look of disbelief. This small series of actions is very quick but unmistakable to those who observe it.

Facial expressions

All of our verbal language is supported by our facial expressions. If we say that we are depressed, for example, we are likely also to be wearing a miserable face. You can tell by their expression that someone is afraid.[22] The statement that we are furious will be accompanied by a glaring, angry expression. If you were to tell someone that you hated them while wearing a happy beaming smile on your face, both of you would burst into laughter – which just goes to show that body language can be so much more powerful than the spoken word.

Human beings have the most developed set of facial muscles in the animal kingdom, and it follows that our facial expressions are the most complex and varied, even among primates. According to researchers Eckman and Friesen, there

23

24

25

are six basic facial expressions that are commonly used and understood by all peoples and cultures. These expressions reflect:

- happiness
- disgust[23]
- sadness
- anger
- fear
- interest

When we are children, our expressions are free-flowing and uninhibited because we have not fully developed emotional control. As we grow older, we learn emotional restraint and tend to restrict our facial expressions. This process is deemed to be an essential part of growing up.

Our face is our most expressive vehicle in body language, indicating moods, feelings and thoughts. When we are communicating, it is the first part of the body we look at. A genuine smile makes us feel at ease, a sad face may trigger our compassion and an angry face will deter us from approaching. A person who purposefully makes an effort to be devoid of facial expressions can be uncomfortable to be around. They wield a power over us because we cannot interpret much of what they are thinking and feeling. A person with a dry wit or a sense of irony may also be difficult to come to terms with, as their cutting humour will be accompanied not by the expected smile and twinkling eyes but by a serious facial expression.

The smile

One of our most frequently used and striking expressions is the smile. A warm smile can alter moods and change attitudes, and has the power to make us feel better about ourselves and the world around us.

Not all smiles, however, are frank and inviting. The different types encompass:

- A sneer[24]
- A leer
- A sarcastic smile
- A warm, genuine smile[25]

- A sinister smile
- A cheesy, false smile
- A grin[26]
- A beaming smile[27]
- A laugh

Exercise: The effects of a smile

Make a conscious effort to smile more today. Make this a happy loving smile and direct it especially to people you would not normally give the time of day to. Try smiling at everyone you come into contact with – the ticket-seller at the train station, the cashier in the supermarket and so on. Try smiling even when you are complaining.

Make a note of how smiling changes your feelings and whether your smile has any effect on those you are sharing it with. Notice whether it has made your day different from usual. Some things you might notice are that:

- People smile back
- Your day seems easier and less stressful
- You tend to get your own way
- Conversations last longer
- You get to know people better
- You discover more information
- People go out of their way to talk to you
- Relationships go better
- You receive more sexual advances
- People are more helpful
- You feel happier
- Your day is more fulfilling
- You cope with people better
- Your stress levels are lower
- You see the funny side of things
- You like people more
- You resolve differences with people you didn't think you liked

A smiling face makes everyone feel happy. Laughter is the best exercise for your face and soul.[28]

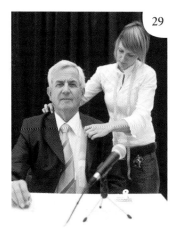

29

Remaining expressionless

In some professions – those where personal feelings would be intrusive or unhelpful – it is necessary to withhold facial expressions. Imagine how you would feel if the television newsreader (whose role is the neutral communication of information) suddenly burst into laughter – or into tears – in response to a news item! These professions include:

- Service (for example, working as a doorman or on a reception desk)
- Newsreading[29]
- Politics
- Undertaking
- Poker playing
- Diplomacy

30

There are times when we need to keep our feelings to ourselves and not to display them to others.[30]

Facial disguise

There are times when we feel over-exposed and do not want the world to see us as we are. In a certain era of the silver screen the great Hollywood stars, such as Marilyn Monroe, Greta Garbo and Frank Sinatra, would often be seen wearing dark glasses and other disguises in order to try to hide themselves from prying eyes. Worn in the right context, dark glasses can provide an aura of mystery and give you a chic look.[31] Worn inappropriately, they can make you an object of ridicule – for instance, if you wear them to go out clubbing at night!

31

Glasses are worn to improve the eyesight; inadvertently, however, they can create a barrier, restricting other people's view of our eyes. In recent years much effort has gone into minimising this barrier, and frames are now much thinner and lenses much lighter than they were in the past. Contact lenses, of course, do away with the barrier completely, and we have now moved into the era of corrective laser eye surgery, which, in some cases, can help to restore not only perfect eyesight but also perfect eye contact.

32

Make-up

As well as enhancing our beauty, make-up can also be used as a means of disguise. A woman who wears a lot of make-up is often considered to be 'tarty'.[32] It seems to me, however, that sometimes women wear heavy make-up in order to cover up their vulnerability and show a hard exterior to the world. This is sometimes true of people who wear Goth or Emo make-up.[33] Heavy make-up can also give a falsely aggressive impression, which may be done deliberately as affording a level of self protection.[34]

33

Theatre actors rely heavily on stage make-up to help define their character, to reflect the times in which the play is set and to make themselves look younger or older as necessary. As a child I was fascinated by the circus but terrified of the clowns. I found their make-up sinister and grotesque, perhaps because it hid their real faces. Clowns have featured in many horror movies, so perhaps this sense of unease is universal.[35]

34

While at the Edinburgh Festival performing my one-woman show, I spent my free hours discovering the delights of this ancient city. While crossing a road one day, I came across an elderly lady. Her face was heavily dusted with powder, the reddest of red lipstick was smeared over her lip line and she wore bright red blusher on her cheeks. She looked like a painted doll, and I couldn't help but smile at her. Noticing my smile, she asked me if I would help her across the busy road, which I happily did. She proceeded to inform me that her eyesight was 'most blurry these days'. I realised that when she looked into her mirror, she saw very little indeed and so just went on applying make-up until she was satisfied.

35

36

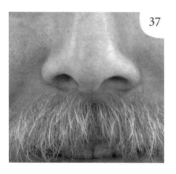

37

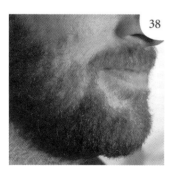

38

39

Facial hair

For men in particular, facial hair is a great form of disguise. However, it can also be used to express personality traits.

Eyebrows

Eyebrows frame the eyes and can be used to make some wonderfully silly expressions. Actors portraying frightening and sinister characters in pantomime and on the silver screen frequently use eyebrow movements.[36] The bushier your eyebrows are, the more eccentric and wild your appearance becomes. Some amazing characters have had eyebrows that are a striking feature, for example astronomer Patrick Moore; politicians Dennis Healey, Michael Foot and Disraeli; and the painter Frida Kahlo, whose eyebrows, which joined in the middle to make the shape of a bird's wings, were a trademark feature often depicted in self-portraits.

Moustaches

A moustache often indicates a stiff upper lip. Personally, I never trust a man with a moustache. It gives me the impression that he is emotionally rigid and chauvinistic or that he is hiding something, but that is just a personal feeling and may relate to individual experiences.[37]

Beards

Like a moustache, a beard suggests to me that a man has something to hide, since a beard effectively conceals many facial expressions. Men with very neat beards have a tendency to be fastidious, with an over-zealous attention to detail.[38] A large or unkempt beard suggests a man who refuses to conform, is comfortable with himself and cares not a jot for the opinion of others. A goatee beard – trendy, thin and precision-cut – gives an air of chic and refinement, but do not be hoodwinked. This is a guy who is not only fastidious but who also has an extremely inflated opinion of himself. He will probably believe that he is the world's greatest lover – sadly, this is an illusion![39]

The eyes have it

The eyes are one of our most powerful and most revealing body language tools – the truth can always be found in them, regardless of the messages our facial expression and words are giving out. We may act as if we are happy, we may appear to be interested, we may put on a smiling face, but if our eyes do not paint the same picture, they will give us away.

A simple look can express:

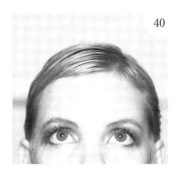

- disinterest[40]
- sex appeal[41]
- challenge[42]
- fear[43]

or a myriad of other emotions.

The pupils

Throughout history the eyes have frequently been decorated, highlighted and enhanced to give an impression of beauty, mystique and expressiveness. One of the more extreme attempts to do this involved the use of the poisonous herb belladonna to dilate the pupils. We tend to find enlarged pupils beautiful, just as we tend to feel uncomfortable around and shy away from cold, staring beady eyes. The pupils dilate naturally when we see someone we are attracted to or something that pleases us. When lovers gaze into each other's eyes, their pupils become highly dilated. This dilation leads to further sexual arousal and locks the lovers into a transfixed, intimate gaze. Another reason for our attraction to enlarged pupils is that babies and young animals naturally have them. This appealing trait is designed to increase their chances of survival, assuring them of care and nurture from adults of the species.

Light conditions also affect the dilation of our pupils. If we are in the dark or semi-dark, our pupils will dilate in order to let in as much light as possible so that we can see. If we are exposed to bright light or natural sunshine, our pupils will contract in order to protect themselves. These actions are beyond our control.

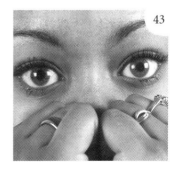

44

45

In normal light conditions, however, the pupils contract and dilate as we experience certain thoughts and feelings. If we have negative thoughts or if something does not please us, our pupils contract. If we have positive feelings or are excited, our pupils dilate. These reactions, too, are beyond our conscious control, and we can therefore glean a considerable amount of information about another person's state of mind from observing them, although one should always do so subtly.

Social eye contact

In a social situation it is natural for us to look around and assess the people nearby. Our eyes focus on people we find attractive or interesting, and all the while we are making judgements and storing information about them. It is said colloquially that attention from someone attractive or important can 'turn our heads'. This is indeed physically the case. If someone we admire catches our eye, we will turn our head to look at them. We also automatically look at people when they enter or leave a room. This is why walking into a room alone can be a daunting and uncomfortable experience.

During normal conversation, eye contact is intermittent.[44] Maintaining a constant gaze would be uncomfortable and unnatural. The person who is doing the talking will periodically look away, as if giving thought to what they are saying, and then return to eye contact in order to confirm that the other person is listening and understands what is being said. The listener will look at the speaker far more frequently if they are interested in what is being said.[45] If they are distracted or bored, they will make minimal eye contact. If their attention is totally lost, they will look away.

Considerably more eye contact is made when people are facing each other than when they are sitting side by side, so if you want to engage someone in what you have to say, sit directly opposite them.

Being watched

As children we are told that 'it's rude to stare'; this is because staring is usually an aggressive act.[46] We find being watched an uncomfortable experience. It can knock our confidence and make us feel self-conscious. If the watching continues, our instinctive interpretation is that we are in a potentially dangerous situation. Does the person staring at us wish us harm, dislike us, find us sexually attractive ...? Sexual staring, although not overtly aggressive, can be disconcerting, especially if the attraction is not reciprocated. A person who finds us attractive will usually make other obvious gestures such as a smile, a raise of the eyebrow or even a blown kiss.

46

We do not feel unnerved, however, if a small child stares at us, as they are hardly likely to pose a threat and are probably just inquisitive.[47] Moreover, they have not yet learnt adult rules about eye contact.

47

Giving the right eye signals

The further away you are from someone, the easier it is to keep eye contact and the less imposing your visual contact will be. The closer you are, the more likely you are to break eye contact and alter your gaze patterns.

Too little eye contact suggests disinterest or boredom and is deemed to be rude. Shyness can also cause us to avoid making eye contact (inadvertently causing a negative reaction). Closing the eyes completely when speaking is another negative signal, suggesting that we are afraid to look and would rather block out an uncomfortable experience.[48]

48

Trying to have a conversation with a person who is avoiding looking at you can be a frustrating experience. A possible way to overcome this is to ask a question, which may encourage the other party to make more of a connection with you. A persistent refusal to look you in the eye may suggest that the person you are talking to is lying to you or being evasive. Try asking them to 'look me in the eye and say that', as to lie while making eye contact is very difficult. Whenever my husband is avoiding telling me the whole story, I get him to look me in the eye and then he invariably bursts out laughing with embarrassment.

Too much eye contact, on the other hand, can make the other person feel uncomfortable. Excessive eye contact connotes an invasion of their privacy and suggests scrutiny.

49

Read my eyes

We sometimes stare someone in the eye when we feel unable to speak for fear of being overheard but want them to read our minds. We do this with close friends and loved ones – those who we feel should be able to guess what we are thinking.

Official eye contact

50

During business meetings and serious conversations, keeping your gaze to an official format is vital. Indeed, where you look is an important factor in maintaining your conversation at the correct pitch. In such a situation you should look at the area around the eyes and forehead, glancing at documents or breaking eye contact occasionally.[49] Moving your gaze any lower than this will alter the tone and seriousness of what is being discussed. A gaze that includes the face will take the conversation on to a much more friendly level, and this should only be done if and when appropriate.[50]

Glancing at someone's cleavage or crotch area would, for obvious reasons, be most inappropriate and would certainly change the emphasis of your conversation. Most women will know how infuriating it is to be trying to have a serious conversation with someone who is transfixed by your bosom or the comely shape of your legs!

Friends and casual gaze

In more relaxed situations, with friends and people you know, your gaze will take in more of a person's face. This social gaze incorporates the whole of the face and eyes to as low down as the lip and mouth area. This form of eye contact is acceptable with someone you feel comfortable with and with whom you are having a friendly discussion.

Intimate gaze

51

Discovering if someone is 'giving you the eye' is a simple matter. Be aware of where they are looking at you. If they fancy you, their gaze will move from your eyes, linger around your lips and mouth, and occasionally drop lower to the delicate area around your neck. The look is very seductive, and if both of you are sexually attracted to each other, your eyes will perform this courtship dance together. The look might be somewhat discreet and the glance might only briefly lower to neck and chin level and quickly return to your eyes, but it will be enough for you to know what the other person is really thinking.

Flirting

52

Innocent flirting is normal social behaviour and is a light and friendly interplay of eye contact within the intimate gaze zone. The glances are quick, performed in a spirit of fun, and accompanied by smiles and laughter.[51] Women when flirting tend to flutter their eyelids in order to appear coy and seductive.

More serious flirting is done slowly and with intent. Eye contact will be held longer than normal, and the lowered gaze will be made with purpose.[52] It is also likely to be accompanied by body touch as and when the opportunity presents itself. The body touch may be discreet or it may be downright obvious. Playing with the hair is frequently used to emphasise the sexy looks.[53]

53

To deal with unwanted flirting, keep your eye contact in the business gaze zone, making sure you never look lower than the other person's eye level. This will very soon send the message that you are not interested, and the other person should, with any luck, cease their unwanted attentions.

When strong eye contact can be effective

Direct eye contact is a powerful tool and can speak volumes. Use it to emphasise a point (though be careful not to hold the gaze too intensely as it could be read as an act of aggression). Hold firm eye contact when you have something serious to say or when reprimanding a child, to let them know you mean business.[54] In business meetings and work situations where you are trying to give an impression of assertiveness and confidence, do not be afraid to look people in the eye.[55] If you are making a complaint, a face-to-face encounter will have more impact, and direct eye contact will show that you are not going to back down.[56] Hold a person's gaze if you want them to speak to you, and if you are giving a speech, try to maintain eye contact with as many members of your audience as possible.

54

The eyebrow flash

This universal gesture, in which the eyes momentarily open widely and the eyebrows rise and fall, is performed when we make initial eye contact. It is a form of greeting and acknowledgement of another's presence.

Winking

Winking is one of those delightful old-fashioned gestures that seems to be used only by the older generation these days. A wink signifies a bond between two people and is often used

55

between an adult and a child to imply that they have a secret and are of the same mind. A wink can also be used as a signal between two knowing partners, as seen in the old gangster movies, in which it often signifies time for action.

Another rather old-fashioned gesture is a wink accompanied by a double-clicking noise. This sign was once commonly used by men when they thought a woman looked terrific. It seems to be dying out, presumably because it is considered sexist.

56

Arty or academic?

When breaking eye contact during conversation, we take our eyes either to the left or the right. It is thought that people with artistic and creative temperaments will break their gaze to their left. Those with more academic and lateral-thinking minds tend to break their gaze to their right.

Lips do more than talk

Our lips are one of the most sensual areas of our bodies. We use them for eating and drinking, one of life's greatest pleasures. A kiss is a gesture of our affection and deep feeling – we blow kisses into the air, we kiss our pets, we kiss good friends on the lips, we kiss others on the cheek, we kiss babies and children.[57] The Pope even kisses the ground! When we kiss, the thousands of tiny nerve cells within our lips experience the sensation, from which exudes warmth, love and passion.

57

Tight-lipped

The term 'tight-lipped' is used to describe a person who refuses to talk and will not disclose a certain piece of information. Closing the lips is, of course, a gesture that prohibits speech. Pursing the lips, or pressing them together, is an expression of disapproval that also carries the suggestion of a reluctance to speak.[58] The message is, 'I don't approve of that, but far be it from me to say anything about it'. We often purse our lips and frown when we are deep in thought – often totally unaware that we are doing so.

58

Thin lips

Thin lips can give a person a harsh appearance if they are accompanied by a serious expression. They can sometimes be associated with a personality that is mean, meagre and stern – although I know people with thin lips who totally belie that generalisation! If we are feeling negative, we tend to tighten our lips, giving us that 'pinched look'.

59

If you have naturally thin lips and feel they sometimes give the wrong impression, there are several ways to make them appear fuller. The simplest and most cost-effective way to deal with thin lips is to think positive and smile![59] Otherwise, women can try using a lighter shade of lipstick (the darker the lipstick, the thinner the lips appear), or draw an extended lip line beyond the natural edge of your lips but still following their contours. Lipsticks that contain collagen are now also available. This is said to plump up the lips, giving them a more voluptuous look. Add an extra layer of lip-gloss and the thin-lip look is no more.

60

The pout

The sexy pout is an age-old image that has adorned the front covers of glossy magazines for years. In the long term this has caused women to believe that pouting is the perfect way to look.[60] After breast implants, one of the most popular cosmetic operations is the collagen lip enhancement. An astounding number of female celebrities and models have had this operation done, and these hot lips are allegedly flaunted by the likes of Liz Hurley, Patsy Kensit, Melanie Griffiths and Meg Ryan. Such surgery, however, is not always a resounding success. The English actress Lesley Ash, best known for her role in *Men Behaving Badly*, was cruelly named 'best "trout pout" of the year' by the media after her collagen lip enhancement went badly wrong.

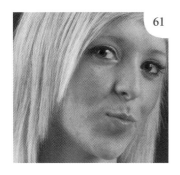

61

The pout is a sensual gesture. According to anthropologists, the lips represent the female genitalia moist and ready for penetration (see page 26). The permanent pout purportedly makes women look more sexually appealing – perhaps because it suggests that they are permanently ready for sex.[61]

Blowing a kiss

We make air-blown kisses as a gesture of affection to a person we care about and to say goodbye. This gesture can also be used to diffuse a potential argument, suggesting that both parties kiss and make up.

62

Biting lips

Taking hold of the lips with the teeth is a sign of nervousness, apprehension and fear.[62] Children often bite their lips when they feel they have done something wrong and are waiting for a reprimand for their actions. This is a gesture frequently used by actors in old black-and-white movies. For instance, a man nervously waiting outside the hospital delivery room will pace up and down, biting his lip.

The tongue

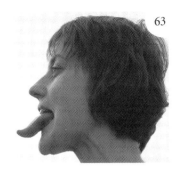

63

Putting your tongue out towards a person is a child-like gesture showing dislike and disdain.[63] It may originate from the refusal to eat more food. The tongue flick is an offensive leery gesture with heavy sexual implications. In *The Silence of the Lambs*, Hannibal Lector's snake-like, licking action made a chilling impact, indicating his pleasure at eating human flesh while at the same time having sexual implications.

Take my hand

Hand gestures range from the flamboyant and elaborate to the minuscule. As we talk we move our hands freely and spontaneously, touching, gesturing and often preening ourselves. When I was at drama school, I recall one of our tutors insisting that if we did not know what to do with our hands, then we should do nothing. We were to deliver lines standing erect with our hands draped loosely by our sides. Now that might look fine if you are delivering a speech on close-up camera, because to move would ruin the shot, but have you ever tried talking with your hands dangling by your side? The result is wooden and restricted, and it makes for a stilted delivery. As we speak, our hands want to move freely in a fluid and natural way.

Some cultures, Indian and Latin, for example, accompany their conversation with energetic hand gestures. The British tend to be more reserved in the way they use their hands.

The handshake

64

Over the years we have developed the handshake as a gesture of formal greeting.[64] Until relatively recently it was mostly restricted to men, being performed by women only of the higher classes (and then relatively infrequently). Times have changed, however, and handshaking has become a regular practice for men and women.

The manner in which a person shakes your hand can provide you with some useful information about their character. For example:

65

- A firm and definite handshake reflects a strong and confident personality.[65]
- An aggressive hand-crunch suggests a dominating, over-powering person who likes to be in control.
- A weak, limp-wristed handshake suggests someone who is detached, withdrawn and fey.
- A hot, sweaty handshake indicates nervousness, fear and uncertainty.

66

67

Be warned, however, that sales and business personnel are often taught to perfect a strong confident handshake in order to create a professional and business-like impression. Such a handshake gives no information as to how they are actually feeling and what their personality is like.

Shaking someone's hand should be a comfortable sensation. If this is not the case, consider what it is that you find uncomfortable. Your conclusion may help you in assessing the person and the situation you find yourself in.

Open hand gesture

A relaxed open hand with the palm facing upwards or outwards indicates receptivity, openness and honesty.[66] It suggests that we want to hear what another person has to say and are keen to establish a trusting relationship with them.

This gesture can be a helpful tool if you need to defuse and calm a tense situation. Let's take a stereotypical scene from a gangster movie. The villain of the piece is holding his victim at gun-point and is threatening to shoot if the police officer comes any closer. The police officer wants to disarm the villain and free his hostage. Dramatic music is playing to further heighten the already tense atmosphere. The policeman slowly approaches, considers his body language and decides on the best and most effective approach. He adopts a calm relaxing tone of voice, opens both hands and shows the empty palms to the villain. This demonstrates that not only is the officer unarmed but that he is honest and can be trusted. As the villain reads this body language and absorbs it, the cynical officer pounces and removes the offending weapon. The villain is now well and truly busted.

So, you see, the open-handed gesture can also be used as a means of deception – and may be accompanied by the words, 'Trust me, I'm telling you the truth'! If this makes you feel uneasy, trust your intuition.

One hand up

A hand held upright with the palm facing outwards means stop.[67] This gesture is often used by officials such as traffic police in order to stop an action. An image of a hand held up in such a way is used on the red light at pedestrian crossings.

Two hands up

Both hands held up to an opponent is a gesture of surrender – frequently seen in movies.

A similar gesture, with a completely different meaning, is the two-handed 'high five', a gesture of mutual congratulation.[68]

Rubbing the hands together

This is a gesture of expectation, excitement and readiness for action. It can also signify a feeling that money may be coming our way. When we are feeling cold, we rub our hands together in order to raise the blood to the skin surface. This, together with the friction, warms the hands up.

Palms pressed together

Hands held gently together in front of the body at chest level give the impression of self-support. This is the humble stance taken by someone being attentive or in quiet contemplation. [69] It is also the hand position assumed for prayer.[70]

Holding hands

We feel comfortable and at ease holding hands with a child.[71] This can be a nurturing, supportive gesture – one of guidance and protection.[72] Lovers hold hands, as may good friends. Holding hands with another adult indicates a certain level of intimacy.

73

74

Clenched hands

Tightly holding one's own hands together indicates an attempt to get a grip on oneself.[73] The more tightly the hands are clenched, the tenser a person is likely to be feeling. Clenched hands are also an indication of some degree of negativity. The higher the hands are clasped in relation to the body, the more negative the person is likely to be. Sitting with elbows resting on a table and hands clenched at face level is an indication of a marked degree of negativity. Hands clenched but supported at table height indicate negativity of a lesser degree. Hands held at thigh level are indicative of slight apprehension rather than blatant negativity.

Clenched fist

A clenched fist is certainly a signal that that a person is frustrated or angry.[76] However, it usually indicates that they are not going to undertake any further action.[74] It expresses threat and frustration rather than an intention of violence.

A clenched fist can also be used in a light-hearted manner to display mild displeasure and annoyance but shows willingness to forgive the other person, hence it is sometimes displayed to a cheeky child. In this case it is accompanied by an expression showing exasperation, which softens the gesture.[75]

75

76

Hands behind the back

This gesture brings a smile to my face, as it vividly brings to mind a picture of my father walking through our garden in this manner. He would stroll contentedly with his hands clasped behind his back, admiring all he surveyed, a king in his own castle. This gesture displays a feeling of confidence and superiority.[77] It is often used in films to characterise captains of industry, doctors, lawyers or people of very high status, such as kings and presidents, in serious contemplation.[78] Yul Brynner perfected it in *The King and I*, in which he was often to be seen pacing up and down with his hands behind his back mulling over yet another regal dilemma put to him by the challenging governess, Miss Anna.

77

Both hands behind the head

This gesture is made by a person who thinks they are better or more knowledgeable than you. They will also tend to lean slightly backwards, thus creating a distance from you, and tilt their head to give the impression that they are looking down their nose at you.[80] One way to deal with this disconcerting posture is to take a similar one yourself. However, this will have the effect of appearing confrontational, which may not be an appropriate way to deal with the situation, especially if the other person is your boss. Nevertheless, it is important to persuade the other person to moderate this intimidating body language, as no headway can be made while they maintain this attitude. Try breaking the negative pattern by leaning into their space and asking a question or changing the subject.[79]

78

79

80

81

Hand grip

In this gesture both hands are behind the back, one with a tight grip on the other. This indicates a person under stress, who is trying to keep a grip on him or herself. The more severe the stress, the tighter the grip will be and the higher up the arm the hold. This gesture can also be seen with the hands in front of the body. It is similar to the crossed arm barrier.[81]

82

Hands over the mouth

When trying to deceive others we often place our hands around or over the mouth area, as if attempting to stop the words tumbling out.[83]

Disguised versions of covering the mouth are the nose touch (see page 162), the eye rub and the ear pull.[82] (For more on lying see Chapter 10.) Interestingly, we also often use this gesture if we disbelieve what someone else is saying to us.[83]

83

Hands over the chest and throat

A gesture that I notice myself and other women using frequently is placing one hand gently over the upper chest and throat area.[84] Occasionally both hands are placed here, depending on the intensity of what is being discussed. Regardless of how well women know one another, we tend to talk to each other on a more intimate and personal level than men usually do, often baring our souls to women we have never met before. This gesture can be seen when women are sharing very personal details. By placing our hand over the delicate upper chest and throat area we are protecting ourselves physically while we speak about emotions or situations that make us feel exposed.

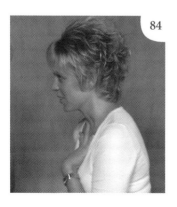

84

Hand movements

Hand movements are used to reinforce speech and are easy to observe in conversation.[85] If you scrutinise the hand actions of politicians, you will see that they use positive and supportive hand gestures demonstratively. Former UK prime minister Tony Blair is an avid user of hand movements. He cuts and slices through the air to put his point across. One of his more dramatic gestures is the two-hand slice: he brings down his hands and bangs them on the table to emphasise the seriousness of his message. Making any hand gesture while maintaining direct eye contact will hold your audience's attention and add impact to whatever you are saying.

They can also be revealing in other ways: straightening your tie ostentationally tells others you feel superior.[86]

Fingers

Fingers are our precision tools; we use them to grip objects in order to accomplish many daily tasks; we use them – and especially the index finger – to point; and we use them to touch. We make many gestures with our fingers, some of which accompany and emphasise the spoken word. We may also use our fingers to signal an insult, using gestures such as the V-sign or tapping the finger against the head (suggesting that another person's brain is not functioning correctly).

Touching fingertips

This gesture suggests an air of confidence and control verging on arrogance, and is often used by a person who is feeling superior.[87] The headmistress at the convent school I attended, Sister Superior Margaretta, would always use this gesture when I had been summoned to her office for chastisement, which I have to admit was on more occasions than I care to remember. I would stand outside her office waiting for the onslaught as she piously looked down her nose at me and intermittently tapped her fingers together. Boy, oh boy, did I know I was in trouble!

Drumming fingertips

We often perform this action when we are thinking, feeling nervous or impatient, or trying to control an inner anger or frustration.[88] In general, the slower and more forceful the finger drum, the more severe the mood. However, drumming away at a fast pace may indicate someone with a nervous disposition who may or may not be aware of this action. We also drum our fingertips absent-mindedly when listening to music and keeping time with the beat – a habit that can be extremely irritating to others.

Pointing

We point to indicate where we would like another person to look.[89] If you are the object of someone's pointing finger, however, it can be an uncomfortable experience and one that may feel threatening in its intent.

A pointing finger used in a prodding manner is a gesture of aggression.[90] Unlike the clenched fist, which is generally a signal of anger that will not be acted on, the pointing finger means business. This gesture is certainly menacing in intent and likely to cause active conflict.

Crossed fingers

We make this gesture of crossed fingers when making a wish or when we have an intense desire for a certain thing to happen and want luck to be on our side.[91] It is likely to have its roots in paganism and resembles making a sign of the cross to ward off the devil.

Steepling fingers

This gesture is generally used by people who feel they are in a position of superiority, or who at least are comfortable with their own status.[92] It is a signal of confidence. It is sometimes used by a boss giving information to an employee. The raised steeple is more common when talking, the lowered steeple when listening.

Fingers in the mouth

When we first come into this world as babies, our cries are responded to initially by the comfort and nourishment of our mother's breast. Children who suck their thumbs are mimicking this action, and will do so in times of stress and need. Adults touch their fingers to their mouths.[93] In adulthood we also sometimes put objects such as pens and pencils into our mouth, in effect reproducing this comfort and reassurance.[94]

Nail biting originates from the same need for comfort which has deteriorated into a compulsion. It is a nervous habit and a form of mild self-harm.

Fingers fiddling with hair

Fiddling with our hair is another form of self-comfort and is often an absent-minded pastime.[95]When being breast-fed or taking their nightly bottle, babies will often twiddle their mother's hair. In general this is a female gesture – perhaps simply because women tend to have longer hair. It is often a combination gesture, linked with biting the lip or other distracted gestures.[96]

97

Thumbs

The thumb represents strength and power, and a protruding thumb is often displayed within a group of other gestures indicative of dominance and aggression. A person standing with their hands in their pockets displaying a protruding thumb is demonstrating a dominant attitude. Women using this stance are showing unequivocal equality with men and strength of character. If this gesture is done with the hands in the back pockets, the attitude is one of superiority that is not on open display.

Be aware of thumb gestures, as they often contradict what a person is saying verbally. The person may be agreeing with you and appearing generally positive, but if they are displaying their thumbs conspicuously, this is a sure giveaway of an aloof and superior attitude. If their arms are also crossed, you can be sure that not only does this person think they are better than you but they are also feeling defensive.

98

Thumbs up and down

We use the thumbs-up sign to give a positive message, such as 'yes', 'all is well' and 'all clear'.[97] We use the thumbs down to give a negative message: 'no', 'all is not well', 'something has gone wrong'.[98]

99

Thumb pointing

Pointing slightly back-handedly with the thumb is a derogatory gesture that makes fun of the person we are pointing at and is often belittling in intent. The message is something like, 'Look at them over there; who do they think they are?' The same gesture can be made with a backward toss of the head.[99]

Arms

We use our arms to make big, dramatic, telegraphic gestures, as opposed to the usually subtler ones that we make with our hands. Arms also express our connectedness with one another; we use them to hug and to hold. At the same time, they express our separateness. With our arms we make defensive barriers between ourselves and other people.

Open arms

The open-armed gesture is a sign of welcome and is often the precursor to an embrace.[100] An open-armed gesture accompanied by a shoulder shrug implies helplessness and is done when a person is in doubt.

Hugging and embracing

We hug ourselves, wrapping our arms around our body, as a form of self-comfort.[101] This posture is often assumed at night in bed, and is accompanied by curled up knees and head bent over, so that we are huddled into a tight ball. This position is assumed by the foetus in the womb and is probably a deeply held body memory. We hug others as a sign of affection. A hug can take the less intimate form of one arm around the other person's shoulder or it may be a full body embrace.[102]

Linking arms

Linking arms with another is a sign of non-sexual friendship and closeness.[103] It also offers physical support (as when walking with an elderly person, for example).

104

Legs

You might think that legs play a minor part in body language, but you would be wrong …

Upright

Standing erect with both feet planted firmly on the ground, or walking with a straight back and purposeful stride suggest alertness and confidence.[104]

105

Open legs

Standing or sitting with the legs open draws the eye line towards the genital area and is a courtship gesture. (See also page 24.)

Straight out

Sitting with your legs held straight out ahead and your body tilted backwards is a sign of boredom and the desire to distance yourself. If this position is taken during conversation, or especially if the hands are behind the head, it suggests arrogance.

106

Crossed legs

Women often cross their legs simply for comfort, changing the direction of the cross when the position becomes uncomfortable.[105] However, crossed legs can also be a defensive barrier, particularly if accompanied by crossed arms.[106] Women also curl their legs underneath them when in a relaxed and intimate conversation.[107] Note in which direction the legs are crossed. If it is away from you, with the foot also pointing away, this indicates a lack of interest. If it is towards you, with the foot also pointing towards you, this indicates interest. (For more information on defensive leg positions see pages 87–8.)

107

Feet

Feet are more than just convenient things to stand on. They play an important role in body language, so pay close attention to what they are doing next time you are involved in people-watching.

Foot-pointing

When standing or sitting, we tend to point our feet towards the person or object of most interest to us.

Foot-tapping

Tapping the foot suggests impatience and the desire to move forwards and get on with things.[108]

Feet planted apart

This stance is usually taken by men, who use it to signal confidence and bravado. It exposes the genitalia and suggests virility and lack of fear. (For more information see page 27.)

Dragging the feet

Dragging the feet suggests reticence and reluctance to engage in an activity or action ahead.[109]

Feet placed on an object

Placing one's feet on a chair, desk or car wheel demonstrates ownership.[110] When you are in a public area (such as a train), placing your feet on the seat opposite you is a forceful way of extending your personal space. This gesture makes the statement, 'Do not sit here; this is mine'.

111

112

Image

The image we present to the outside world is a projection of how we want the world to see us. Within moments of meeting a person for the first time, we make judgements on the basis of their appearance alone. We assess their attractiveness, financial status and occupation, as well as whether they are a threat to us, valuable to us or, indeed, of any importance to us at all. Time will tell how accurate these judgements are.

Clothes

If image is important, clearly the way we dress has a major impact. We have a social dress code and observing it is important if we want to be effective in society.[111] We would never, for example, attend a business meeting in beachwear. That is not so say that we must all dress in an identikit way. It is possible to play the game and retain our individuality to a certain extent, using the dress code creatively to express who we are. Those who do not wish to comply – hippies and travellers for example – soon evolve their own dress code, one that expresses their difference from mainstream society and its values.

Permanent adornments

Body piercing, tattooing and other forms of permanent body decoration can carry many messages. At different times in tribal history, tattooing and body scarring have served as, among other things, a record of dreams and visions, a beautification of the body, a rite of passage and a mark of allegiance signifying belonging to a particular group.[112] These days, however, body piercing and tattooing are being appropriated by the fashion industry. Fashion victims often adopt a particular piece of body art simply because they have seen it on the latest pop idol.

Exercise: Dressing for someone else

113

Use this exercise to find out what impact dressing in a particular way has on how you feel and behave.

- Ask your partner, lover, best friend or parents how they would like you to dress. Now make a big effort to dress to please them.[113]
- How does dressing this way make you feel? Do you behave differently in your new clothes? Do you feel differently about yourself? Does your body language change to go with your clothes?
- If you like, you can use your new insights to adapt your regular way of dressing or even to create a totally new image for yourself.

Exercise: Break the rules

- Choose a forthcoming event to attend completely inappropriately dressed. Go on, if you dare! Go to a pop concert in a pin-striped suit or a wedding in a bikini. Visit a quiet country pub dressed as a Goth, all in black, with a whitened face, black eyes, facial studs and so on.[114]
- How did this feel? Did it make you feel vibrantly alive, a true rebel, or was it an uncomfortable experience? Would you rather play safe in life or did breaking the conventions give you a buzz?

114

115

116

117

118

Props

Props are items such as bags, glasses, cigarettes and so on that we use either to support us emotionally or in order to achieve a particular effect.

One of the most frequently used props is the cigarette. When feeling nervous, uncomfortable and in need of reassurance, many of us reach for one. It takes our minds off the situation, calms us down and gives us something to do with our hands – a perfect displacement activity. The way a smoker blows smoke can be an indication of the way they are feeling.[115] Blowing smoke upwards shows confidence and assurance, while blowing it downwards demonstrates negativity and anger.[116] A macho way of smoking is to hold the cigarette tightly pinched between two fingers, inhale firmly, aggressively blow the smoke out downwards, throw the cigarette butt on the floor, scrunch it out with a firm foot and walk away – a series of actions performed many times by Clint Eastwood in spaghetti westerns to display silent aggression. The definite and premature extinguishing of the cigarette clearly signals that a decision has been reached.

Cigars are display props of confidence and high status. A girlfriend of mine has a habit of ordering a cigar, snapping it in two and enjoying her smoke. She is without doubt a confident, strong-willed, in-your-face, comfortable-with-herself type of woman.

Drinking glasses and cups make excellent props. Warming your hands on a hot cup of chocolate creates a comfortable barrier and provides warmth with an added feeling of security.[117] Drinking at a bar or social occasion is another supportive displacement activity. Holding the glass gives you something to do with your hands, provides a barrier and thus makes you feel more at ease.

Oral props include pens, pencils, pipes and the arm of our reading glasses. We often place these objects in our mouths when thinking and making decisions.[118] We may also tap our teeth with the object – a sign that we are stalling and need more time to reach a conclusion.

Bags, books, mobile phones or anything else we can hold in our hands may be used as a protective barrier and an emotional prop. This kind of prop is often used as an extension of our hands. We point with sticks, slap faces with gloves and raise our glasses to offer someone a drink.

Touch

For many years the British have been considered less tactile than people in other European countries. Only in the last 20 years or so has greeting someone with a kiss become an acceptable form of greeting in Britain – a habit picked up from our more touch-oriented European friends.

119

Touching another person, in other than an aggressive way, implies there is a connection of some kind. Some employers have realised the benefits of the power of touch and now send employees on bonding activities where group hugs are encouraged among participants.

The sense of touch is so vital to our well-being and growth that babies and young animals will die if they are deprived of it.[119] Children are calmed and reassured by it.[120] Any form of touch – be it a tender caress or jostling in a busy crowd – will cause some stirring or reaction in us, since our skin is the most sensitive part of our bodies. It has been observed that when we stroke a pet our blood pressure drops and we become calmer. Nursing homes for the elderly and children's hospitals often encourage visits by people with pets, knowing that physical contact with animals can have a beneficial effect on their residents.

120

Touch and ownership

Touch is also used to display ownership.[121] My local gym is run by a pair of young, newly married and rather attractive instructors. As I was leaving after one of my recent visits, I had to pass a group of older women who were gathered around the male instructor following an energetic aerobics class. They were flirting and he was enjoying every moment! When this scene was noticed by his wife, she immediately came out to join the group. She made a beeline for her husband and, with a big smile on her face, put her arm firmly around his shoulder, announcing to the group through her body language that this was her man so, 'Hands off, girls'. We behave in much the same way with our possessions. We claim our ownership by leaning on our cars, putting our feet up on our chairs and sprawling happily all over the things we own.

121

122

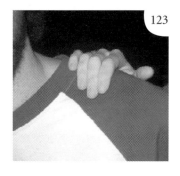

123

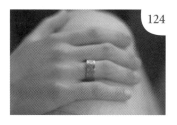

124

125

Touch and taboo

Of course, there are areas of the body that are taboo to touch. The sexual zones are restricted to lovers, and invasion of them by anyone else is usually a very traumatic event.[122] The areas we allow others to touch are the head, hands, arms and back.[123]

Recently my husband and I were sitting together on bar stools in our local village pub having a quiet drink. A mutual male friend joined us. In the course of the conversation he gripped me fairly hard on the thigh, just above the knee.[124] I guess it was the nearest part of my anatomy to him, but I felt it was a totally inappropriate place to touch me, especially as I was wearing a short skirt at the time. The conversation carried on as normal, and both he and my husband were oblivious to what had just occurred, and so I let it go without comment. I was almost sure there was no sexual motive – or was there? I made my excuses and slipped out to the restroom to cool down. I was angry at what had just happened and was not sure how to deal with it. I decided to remain standing when I returned to the bar. That way temptation was well and truly out of the way.

People who abuse the unspoken laws of the etiquette of touch are disliked and very quickly earn themselves the reputation of being a groper. It is inappropriate to touch someone in a friendly and intimate way if you have never met them before, and even with people you do know it is important to keep within the accepted touch zones. We know these instinctively, and a person who abuses them is fully aware of what they are doing.

In some professional capacities, of course, touching is totally acceptable and expected.[125] This is the case in nursing and in teaching sports. In most situations we tend to excuse accidental touching, which can be unavoidable in crowded public places. Nevertheless, even an accidental touch does not go unnoticed.

Social touch

The degree to which we desire to establish appropriate body contact with someone is a measure of how much we like them. (The saying 'I wouldn't touch him with a barge pole' expresses the negative end of this continuum.) When we are introduced to a person for the first time, formal touch is usually established in the form of a handshake. As you begin to open up and relax, this initial formality may be dropped for a somewhat friendlier approach and you may begin to make light physical contact such as touching an arm or patting a shoulder.[126] By the time you are parting, a formal handshake may feel inappropriate and a kiss on the cheek or hug more fitting. If you have not connected, however, another formal handshake will do just fine.

126

The more extrovert and outgoing a person is, the more likely they are to be a 'touchy' person.[127] Reaching out and touching appropriately can make you more popular, more accessible and more approachable to others. If you are a shy person by nature, you are unlikely to feel comfortable touching others. If this is the case, try experimenting with friendly touching. It is quite possible to develop confidence with touch if you weren't born with it or were brought up to touch only in a restrained way.

127

Touch to support and comfort

We touch others when we wish to offer them support and encouragement.[128] This could be when a person is about to take on a challenge, for example running the marathon or going for a job interview. Alternatively it could be when someone is feeling emotionally down or physically weak. A strong firm arm can be a tower of strength in such a situation, offering reassurance, boosting morale and giving comfort.

128

129 Exercise: Heighten your awareness of touch

- Next time someone touches you, pause discreetly and tune in to the sensation. Note on what part of the body you have been touched and by whom.
- Now notice how this particular touch makes you feel. For example, a pat on the head, holding a hand or a ruffle of the hair may make you revert momentarily to childhood – that may be pleasant or infuriatingly patronising, depending on the circumstances.[129] A rub on the back may feel comforting and supportive. A friend linking arms with you may feel intimate and reassuring.[130]

130

3 Get Out of My Space

Human beings are very social animals and we sometimes share restricted domestic, work and wider territories with many other people. An important factor in maintaining harmony within such dense groups is respect for personal space. By adhering to unspoken rules of behaviour about who gets what space and when, we are able to live in relative peace and uphold social order. Central to all of this is our ability to use body language to signal our need for space, our ownership of our territory, our guest status on someone else's territory and the multitude of other subtle messages that we need to communicate in order to live together with other human beings.

The four body zones

In general terms, personal space can be divided up into four categories, starting with the most intimate and moving outwards to the more public. These categories are a general guide. In reality they vary slightly from person to person, and may also vary significantly from culture to culture.

Inner intimate zone

This zone extends from body contact to approximately 15 cm (6 in). It is reserved for lovers, very close friends, parents and children.[1] When a person is invited into this space zone, we give them permission to touch our skin – a highly sensitive part of our anatomy.[2] If we are touched without having given permission, we can feel violated.

Touch can communicate many messages, including tenderness, comfort, violence and sexual desire.[3] Imagine that a couple have had a heated argument. One of the partners reaches out to touch the other in an attempt to resolve the situation. The affronted party may well say, 'Get away from me ... Don't you touch me!', demonstrating that at that moment, while they remain in conflict, this inner

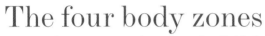

4

5

6

intimate zone is a no-go area.[4] Access to this zone can only be re-established when the rift is over and both parties have given full consent. Of course, this will probably not be articulated in words, but will be negotiated by a series of physical gestures of approach and acceptance until the normal boundaries are restored.[5]

Outer intimate zone

Like the inner intimate zone, the outer intimate zone – as the name suggests – is an area that only such people as members of our family, close friends and lovers have access to. It extends from approximately 15 cm (6 in) to approximately 45 cm (18 in).

While in the most intimate zone, however, touch is allowed, the outer intimate zone permits close proximity but not physical contact.[7] As with the inner zone, anyone entering this zone without our consent can cause a multitude of adverse reactions, both mental and physical. As our safety and self-protection mechanisms automatically click into gear, our blood pressure increases, as does our adrenalin level. The hair on the back of our neck rises and our skin tightens. We either back off, move out of the way or close ourselves in completely – as we might do on entering a crowded lift in which it is virtually impossible to avoid physical contact with others but where we behave as though we are on our own.[6]

7

There are some exceptional situations in which we allow strangers into our outer intimate zone. These include crowded clubs and bars, meetings or lectures.[10] They also cover lifts, and buses and underground trains.[8] Nevertheless, there are limits to the degree of physical intimacy that we will accept even in these situations.[9]

Several years ago I was standing on an overcrowded bus. It was a hot day and I was with a family group, all taking the chaotic ride in good humour. Until, that is, a man standing opposite looked me right in the eye and moved up closer to me. He slid his hand behind my back and took a good handful of my bottom! I was incensed. My reaction was instantaneous: I slapped him across the face. (Perhaps he thought that because I was speaking English, I also had a phlegmatic English temperament; actually I am half-Italian and have a fiery personality to match.) He had violated not only my outer intimate zone (who could help that on the crowded bus?) but also my inner intimate zone, and I was certainly affronted by it. By the end of the day I was able to find this rather trivial incident amusing. However, it is easy to understand how people who have been subjected to crimes of violence often need many years to come to terms with such extreme violation.

11

12

13

In our hectic modern lives, we are often prepared to sacrifice personal space temporarily in order to save time. Thus when we enter a confined space such as a bus, underground train or lift, we make the necessary adaptations in our body zones. In a crowded lift, for example, in order to the preserve personal space we may behave as if no one else is there, looking up at the ceiling or down at floor, or becoming transfixed by the lighted floor numbers as the painful seconds tick by.[11] When we walk out of the lift, our personal space zone reverts to normal.

Many years ago, I moved from the relatively spacious city of Manchester down south to an overcrowded London. In general, people in the north of England are more chatty and approachable than people in the south. As I travelled around on public transport, at first I was very surprised at all the blank (and what I took to be miserable) faces I saw around me. I smiled at people and tried to strike up conversations with them, but there was little response and I soon gave up, disconcerted by being constantly blanked out and ignored. After a while, however, I began to see that the behaviour of people on London buses was due not to the fact that Londoners are inherently rude and unfriendly but to the daily bombardment of their personal space caused by the high population within the confines of the city. In response their natural reaction was to shut down and withdraw into themselves. By avoiding eye contact, making no attempt at conversation and acting as if the other people around them did not exist, they were in fact preserving what they could of their limited personal space.

Next time you make a journey on a train or bus, make a note of where you sit down and how you make yourself comfortable. Notice whether you (or any of the other passengers) spread out or place your bags and belongings on the seat next to you.[12] This commonplace action is in fact intended to extend, if only for a short while, your outer intimate zone. It is a message to anyone thinking about sitting near you not to encroach too closely.[13] Of course, when other passengers see your belongings placed on another seat, they are perfectly aware that no one is sitting there; however, they will usually respect your marking out of personal space, and if other seats are available will walk by and sit elsewhere.

If no other seats are vacant, then, reluctantly, they will approach the seat containing your belongings and ask permission to sit down.[14]

The urge to protect our space is a natural and fundamental survival instinct. All animal life forms mark and defend their territory, and woe betide any other creature who decides to invade it. While we may be sophisticated animals who live in overcrowded cities, we have not lost our territorial instinct. The lack of space in the urban environment and the frequent personal intrusions that result play a major role in creating stress, often resulting in incidents of violence and aggressive behaviour. In rural areas where the population density is much lower and personal space is less of an issue, such violence and aggression is less common.

Personal zone

Extending beyond our intimate zone is our personal zone, which extends from approximately 45 cm (18 in) to approximately 1.2 m (48 in). This is the distance we will stand comfortably apart from people with whom we are familiar, such as work colleagues, friends at the pub and acquaintances at informal gatherings.[15] At this distance we can easily move in and out of other people's inner and outer intimate zones temporarily, having been given tacit permission. We may do this to shake hands, to touch someone in jest, to give someone a reassuring squeeze on the arm or pat on the shoulder, or to plant a welcoming kiss. Between friends this movement into a more intimate zone is generally comfortable and acceptable.

Notice, however, the way people react when a stranger is welcomed into the group. The dynamics almost invariably change, with the personal zone opening out to accommodate the new person. If the person is not known, it is likely that some form of greeting and introduction will take place. Barrier

16

gestures may initially be adopted, such as crossing an arm or holding a hand in front of the body.[16] If the person is viewed suspiciously, barrier gestures may intensify, with arms being folded and legs and ankles crossed (see pages 86–8). Some individuals may take a step backwards to adjust their personal space; others may turn a cold shoulder or turn their head completely away to talk to someone else. It is possible that someone will make an excuse to leave – to go to the toilet, for example. If the newcomer is accepted, however, the barriers will slowly come down and the group will begin to move closer together once again, resuming normal conversation.

Social zone

When we are among people we are not so familiar with, our body zone becomes greater still. Our social zone extends from approximately 1.2 m (48 in) to approximately 3.6 m (12 ft). Strangers are not allowed to stand as close to us as a friend is, and we are immediately on alert if a stranger intrudes into our personal zone.[17] There are, however, many everyday situations – such as buying something in a shop, dealing with a plumber or showing your bus ticket to an inspector – that call for us to interact with people we do not know.

17

As you go about your day, make a mental note of the distance people you do not know stand away from you when such an interaction occurs. As you become more familiar with some of these people (for example, a shopkeeper who serves you every day), notice whether this distance changes. Distance is often a yardstick by which to measure the strength of the relationship you have with a particular person. Simply put, the closer they stand to you physically, the closer they are to you emotionally. As a stranger starts to become more of a friend, the distance comfortably maintained between you during communication will become smaller as you let each other into your life and your space.

Public arena

This body zone comes into use when we are addressing a group of people – for example, giving a speech, teaching in a formal situation or leading a workshop – and spreads over approximately 3.6 m (12 ft). In order that everyone can see and hear us, in this situation we will naturally stand at a distance of about 3.6 m (12 ft) away from our audience.[18] However, if the group we are addressing is quite small, the gap will also be smaller; in a seminar for example.[19] If the group is much larger, as in a classroom, on the other hand, the gap will be correspondingly larger so that contact is maintained with everyone.[20]

When I was performing my one-woman show *Magic Moments* at the Edinburgh festival, I noticed that my performance would change if there was a full house. The theatre where I was playing was compact to say the least, and when it was full, the audience would be sitting less than a metre away from me, right under my nose and in my face. This was quite intimidating for both myself and the people in the front row – indeed, only the bravest of souls would venture there, as subconsciously they knew they were going to impinge upon my personal space. The show was aptly described as an 'intimate performance'.

Cultural differences in body zones

The personal space zones I have been discussing relate primarily to English-speaking, Western nations, and people from other cultures often have slightly different body zones. Although the difference may be only slight, our intuitive sense of personal space is acute, and even this kind of minor disparity can be enough to make conversation uneasy. If you find yourself in such a situation, you may be aware that something is wrong but unsure quite what. If you are coming into contact with people from a particular culture for the first time, a few enquiries into their local customs and etiquette could avoid potential embarrassment.

When a person stands just that bit too close to you, it can make you feel very uncomfortable. The natural reaction is to take a step backwards to adjust to the right space for

you.[21] If, however, the other person comes from a nation that has smaller body space zones, they may want to move closer again. This can be the beginning of an unwanted dance routine, with the two of you manoeuvring around the room, you edging backwards and the other person creeping forwards! It is understandable if the person from the larger body zone culture forms the misapprehension that the other person is making sexual advances towards them.

People from Latin countries, such as Italy and Spain, are generally more tactile than the reserved British or Germans. Not surprisingly, their body space zones tend to be slightly smaller too, as I have discovered on occasion. Perhaps surprisingly, the Danes also have notably small body space zones and use eye contact more readily. Far Eastern nations have even smaller body space zones. In many cities in India, such as Delhi or Mumbai, personal space zones are practically non-existent.[22] On my travels there, I quickly had to accept a new definition of my own personal space.

Extended personal space and territorial behaviour

23

Our personal space extends to our homes. Here we make a point of defining our space by marking out boundaries with hedges and fences. Our home is our castle.[23] This is where we feel safe, protected and in control. We dominate our space and are the master of it.

24

Within our working environment, too, we will strive to create and establish our personal boundaries in a similar fashion.[24] The original concept of open-plan office design was intended to maximise the use of floor space. Whoever came up with this idea did not take human nature into account. People require and are prepared to fight for personal space. The typical open-plan office is a war zone in which the object of the battle is territory. Shields, barriers and screens are erected in order to mark the boundaries of people's individual quarters. Where such barriers are not possible, demarcation lines are established with anything that comes to hand – stacks of files, piles of books, phones, staplers, clothes ... You name it and it will be used to define the ownership of space.[25]

25

We also incorporate items that we own into our personal space: our desk or working area, or our car being perhaps the most notable example. We command the space not only within the confines of our car but also the area immediately surrounding it. Any other vehicle that comes too close will be seen as a personal threat. This is why we react with rage when another vehicle drives right behind us, forces us to swerve, overtakes too fast or steals our parking space. They are attacking our personal space, and we react accordingly. Our pulse rate, blood pressure and adrenalin levels rise, and we are ready for counter-attack. Hence, with car ownership soaring and roads becoming ever more jam-packed with cars, the third-millennium phenomenon of road rage has emerged.

26

Hiding behind your defences

When we are feeling open, confident and comfortable with ourselves, we hold an open body posture. We stand or sit upright with heart and chest exposed, letting the world know that we have nothing to hide.[26] When we feel challenged, however – for example if we are in a situation we do not like, or if we disagree with something that is being said, or even if a negative thought or feeling flits through our mind – we will adopt a more defensive posture. Our body may curve in on itself and we will put up a variety of barriers between the outside world and ourselves.

Arm barriers

27

We fold our arms as a gesture of self-protection, creating a barrier that is in effect shielding our chest and heart.[27] This gesture tends to keep people at bay. Notice when you fold your arms, and consider what might be making you feel defensive. Though you may think that this is simply a comfortable way to sit or stand, research shows that in most cases folded arms are instigated by a negative thought that leads us to want, temporarily, to keep people at a distance. Of course, this can be a constructive strategy in some situations.

A subtle variation on folded arms is the single-arm barrier, in which one arm is folded across the body. We use this when we are feeling slightly uneasy in a social situation. For extra reassurance we may hold our other arm. The advantage of the single-arm barrier is that, unlike folded arms, it is not conspicuous and therefore does not give away the fact that we are feeling uncomfortable.

For women, a handbag can be a defensive prop, or we can use other props such as files or papers.[28] Held with both hands in front of the body, it creates a well disguised barrier for those uncomfortable social moments, such as when entering a room alone or being in strange company, when we may feel exposed. If we are simply feeling a little self-conscious, a handbag can give us the support of something to hold and something to do with our hands.

28

A very subtle variation on the arm barrier, which is often used by men, is the sleeve tug – a brief adjustment of clothing that conveniently and subtly creates a momentary barrier across the body. This gesture is often seen just before an important occasion such as giving a speech. Perhaps the best-known user of this gesture is Britain's Prince Charles, who can frequently be seen tugging at his cuff. A variation on this gesture is checking a watch, which serves the same defensive purpose.

Leg barriers

When crossed arms are accompanied by crossed legs, all the defences are up and channels of communication are closed. Whereas the arms guard the heart, the legs, of course, defend the genital area.

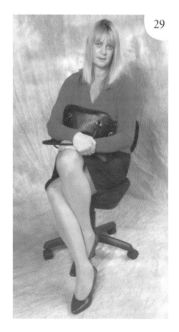
29

For women, however, demurely crossing the legs can simply be a habitual way of sitting, especially if wearing a skirt, and this must be taken into consideration before concluding that a woman is being defensive. Always remember to relate your observations to context and circumstances.

A leg position that almost always implies a defensive attitude, however, is the double leg lock.[29] Here the foot of the crossed leg is hooked around the other leg when seated. You are certainly not going to make much headway with a woman seated in such a way, especially if you have romantic or sexual interests.

30

The ankle cross is a subtle leg barrier that can be used either sitting or standing and is easily disguised. Do take into account, however, that crossing the ankles is a comfortable position if we are sitting for any length of time – particularly if we are relaxed. The ankle cross is likely to be a defensive gesture if used in active conversation while standing.

Next time you are in a social situation, notice who has adopted one of these defensive leg barriers and observe who they are in conversation with. What does this body language suggest about their relationships? This observational information can be especially interesting if you know the people you are watching.

Meeting and greeting

31

We perform an elaborate array of ritualistic behaviour when meeting and greeting the most common being the ubiquitous handshake.[30] We see this greeting all over the world.[31] The closer we are, the more intimate the greeting.[32]

We have probably all had the experience of being among a group of friends when a newcomer enters the group and, for whatever reason, we are not introduced to them. It is a most disconcerting feeling. We will probably feel inhibited in making eye contact and will tend to avoid joining in any conversation until we are introduced or introduce ourselves. Introduction and greeting are part of our social etiquette and formally open the lines of communication.

32

Human body language includes a very wide range of possibilities for greeting, each one geared to a different degree of intimacy. These include:

33

- A nod of the head[33]
- A wink of the eye
- An upheld palm
- A handshake[34]
- A wave of the hand[35]
- A handshake and a pat on the shoulder
- Air-blown kisses and light holding of the shoulders
- A kiss on one cheek
- A kiss on two cheeks (if in France)
- Three kisses (if they really like you)
- A hug
- A twist of the cheek (painful! – Italian greeting of a child)
- A ruffle of the hair
- A pat on the head
- A kiss on the lips[36]
- A long, lingering, hip-hugging kiss
- A high five[37]
- An elaborate high five with several hand twists
- A private group/cult sign (such as a Masonic handshake)
- An army salute
- Nose rubbing (an Inuit and Maori greeting)
- A smile

34

35

36

37

38

Early in human evolution, the smile was actually an aggressive gesture used as a warning to frighten off opponents. This baring of teeth and wide grimace is still used by many animals, such as chimpanzees to warn off unwelcome guests. Throughout the millennia, human beings have adapted and refined the smile until it has become the gesture of greeting that we recognise today.[38] When we pass by a stranger and inadvertently make eye contact, we smile to signal that we do not intend aggression.

However, the smile can also revert to its origins and function as a message of warning. We use this aggressive smile if we are angry with someone or when meeting people we really do not like. The threatening smile gives a clear message to the other person to keep away or suffer the consequences of making any further advances.

39

Parting

Parting has a similar repertoire of ritualistic behaviour. If this ceremony of closure is missing, the parting will feel incomplete. Have you ever had a party guest who, for some reason, went home without saying goodbye? You are left with an odd sensation of something being missing.

Many parting gestures are the same as those for greeting. Parting gestures may vary, however, according to what has occurred during your time in the other person's company. For instance, you may have been introduced to people whom you have got to know well. In this case your parting gesture will probably be more intimate than your gesture of greeting was.[39] On the other hand, you may have had a disagreement with a friend. Naturally your gesture of parting will not be quite as amiable as your greeting.[40]

40

Exercise: Enjoy your own space

In our busy and often stressful world, the need for peace and solitude has never been more urgent. As social creatures we often excel at attending to the needs and demands of others – either in the workplace or at home – but we seldom take time to look after our own needs. We often see time spent alone as empty, unfulfilled and – most frightening of all – lonely; however, spending time alone can be a rich and rewarding experience. Try this exercise to find out how.

- Take yourself out on a date. This can be at any time of the day, but dedicate at least four precious hours to yourself. This is your special treat, so do something you really want to do. Some suggestions include:

    - A trip to the beach[41]
    - A walk in the countryside[42]
    - An outing to a restaurant[43]
    - A trip to the cinema[44]
    - A night in watching a good movie
    - A country drive

45

46

- Spend the time relishing the pleasure of your own company.[45] This is your day or evening out, so if you fancy it, have that big bag of fattening fish and chips and treat yourself to that ice cream.[46] Make some choices and discover what you really like and dislike – in doing so you may get to know yourself better. Most importantly, do not do anything you do not want to do: this is your precious time; indulge in it.

- At the end of the four hours, notice whether there is any change in the way your body feels.

  - Has the tension gone from your shoulders?
  - Have stress lines on your face been replaced by a smile?
  - Do you feel more energised?
  - Is there a bounce in your stride?
  - Is your body language more open?
  - Do you feel more receptive to others?

When I first attempted this exercise, I had great difficulty in spending any time whatsoever in my own company; in fact I found the experience strangely distressing and uncomfortable. I realised I never spent quality time by myself. Several years down the line, I embrace any opportunity to do so.[47]

47

4 I Know What I Want

In this chapter we are going to focus on the kind of body language that will get you what you desire in life – that is, body language that expresses, power, confidence and self-assertiveness. It often appears that random good fortune is the key to success – and in a few cases it is. In general, however, we make our own good fortune by sheer hard work. Having a clearly established picture of a carefully chosen goal, and then applying yourself to the practical measures you need to take to realise it, will open up the gateway for opportunities to come your way.[1] All you need in addition is the right mind-set – one of certainty that you can achieve your ambitions. This certainty will supply you with confidence, a positive attitude, and the energy and enthusiasm to take small but definite steps towards the fulfilment of your dreams.

Start acting as if you have already attained your goal and watch how the world unfolds around you.[2] The world is our mirror, and will respond to us in a way that reflects our energy, beliefs, motivation and outlook. If you are a pessimistic, negative person who believes with a resigned certainty that nothing good ever happens to you, then indeed the universe will almost certainly reflect back to you a life like this. If, on the other hand, you think that life is fun, that everyone around you is friendly and helpful, and that great things are possible, then this is the life that the universe will reflect back.[3]

'I'll believe it when I see it' is a negative axiom; this is not a constructive way to look at life. On the contrary, believe it and then you will see it. Live your life just as you would like to live it, even when difficulties arise, which they invariably will. A positive attitude, even in the darkest of circumstances, will make all these life experiences more bearable. Without doubt life is often challenging. Being constructive and assertive will help you turn challenges into opportunities. Immediately, you will feel in control, rather than a powerless victim of circumstance.

4

5

Exercise: Accomplish what you want

This exercise will help you to work out your immediate priority in terms of what you want to achieve and will prime you to achieve it.

- Just before you go to sleep tonight, choose one thing you would like to accomplish tomorrow. Perhaps it's ringing the girl you met at a party to ask to meet her.[4] It could be visiting the grandchildren you haven't seen for too long.[5]
- Now spend some time imagining yourself doing your chosen task with ease and self-satisfaction. See it in your mind's eye as though it were happening right here and now. Imagine how your body feels as you carry out the task, and make your movements confident, free-flowing and energised.
- In your mind's eye, see your one task accomplished and give yourself a pat on the back. Think how great it will feel when you've delivered that perfect presentation.[6]
- When you get up tomorrow, endeavour to accomplish this task in exactly the way that you imagined it, with the same confidence and the same fluid movements.

Power

Power is being in control, in the driving seat of your life, willing and able to act and make decisions on your own behalf. Power can also influence other people. Money plays an important role in the power stakes and gives us confidence

6

we might otherwise not have. True power, however, is an inner feeling, a strength that draws people to us like a magnet. Power can make things happen. It can be a positive force for good and a destructive force for evil. Power accompanied by the need to dominate through brute force has plagued nations throughout history and continues to be a great concern in the world today.

Confidence

Confidence is maintaining a positive attitude. It has a dynamic energy that cannot help but manifest itself within the body and in body language. A confident person is bold in their actions. (I use the word 'bold' in a positive sense.[7] I once heard a mother chastise her daughter for being 'too bold'! Is that possible?) Even when we are at rest, confidence will still ooze out of us. Confidence is not aggressive and does not shout. Its gestures are strong but not forceful. The energy of confidence is contained and resides within the soul. The body language of a confident person is open and unrestricted, without need for barrier gestures. A confident person is charismatic and a magnet for others.

Self-assertiveness

The more confident a person is, the more assertive they are likely to be. Assertiveness is an active energy and one that you can acquire. In assertiveness training, a person is encouraged to acknowledge their own feelings and then to act upon them constructively. This is an essential step towards improving the quality of your life. Dismissing uncomfortable feelings is self-destructive and turns into resentment, jealousy and bitterness. In the final analysis, it achieves nothing. A submissive person will naturally override their own feelings in favour of those of others. They allow themselves almost willingly to become victims and in doing not only relinquish control of their lives but also leave themselves open to abuse from others. Developing assertiveness is to refuse to be victimised and to take a positive step towards reclaiming your own feelings of self-control and power.[8]

9

Being self-assertive

The following body language traits are used by people who feel powerful and in control. If used sensitively, they will not suggest that you are aggressive or smugly self-confident, simply that you have a sense of your own authority.

Personal space

To give an impression of power, the first and most important thought in your head should be that you have every right to stand on the ground beneath your feet.[9] It is amazing how often we apologise for occupying space. When choosing somewhere to stand or sit, find a space that gives you a view of the whole room. Always sit with your back to a firm wall, as this will give you a feeling of being supported. Position yourself where you can see the entrance to the room.[10] This will make you feel in control, as little can happen without you being aware of it. If you cannot avoid positioning yourself with your back to a door, try to make sure the door is closed. An open door at your back will make you feel unguarded and insecure.

10

Exercise: Own your space

Use this exercise to take possession of the ground that you stand on and the space all around you.

- Place both feet firmly on the ground. Stomp around for a few steps and then, using a definite movement, plant your feet squarely on the ground.
- Take a deep breath and draw the air into the pit of your stomach. Take in as much air as you comfortably can and feel your body weight becoming heavier. This ground you are standing on is now yours and you have every right to occupy it.
- Stretch out your arms and spin round in a full circle as you breathe in. This is your space. Own it! Hold your head up and look the world in the eye. Make no excuses or apologies for being here.[11]
- Take a look all around you and say (out loud or in your head): 'This is my space and I am worthy to be here.'

Try doing a discreet version of this exercise when in a group. You may notice that people instinctively take a step back from you as they sense that you are commanding more space and they are encroaching on it.

Posture

A confident attitude is expressed by a firm, solid upright stance. Stand with both feet planted firmly on the ground. Your back should be erect and your head upright. Look the world in the eye. You should feel the whole weight of your body firmly balanced. Now breathe out and relax – appearing too rigid will have an adverse effect.

Every now and then check your body posture. Make sure you are not slouching and lift up your head. Take your hands out of your pockets and make sure you are not leaning on the furniture. Okay, now smile!

Head position

Keep your head upright and look others squarely in the eye. When trying to look confident, it is a common error to hold the head and nose too high in the air. This conveys arrogance rather than confidence.

12

Facial expressions

The facial expressions you use depend on the situation you are in. A thoughtful look will give the impression that you are considering what is being said and will give you an air of authority and wisdom.[12] If the subject matter is serious, it is appropriate to keep facial expressions to a minimum. On the other hand, remember that confident people smile.

Eye signals

13

Make direct eye contact when speaking.[13] If you are in a group of people, deliver your speech to the person you need to impress the most and also make sure you make eye contact with everyone else. You need to make an impression on everyone, remember. Apart from being unpleasant for the individual concerned, excluding somebody could give an adverse impression. Be careful not to stare, as this will appear confrontational and can make the other person feel intimidated rather than impressed.

Mouth expressions

14

Keep your mouth relaxed. A tight mouth implies anger, and a mouth that is too relaxed appears sexual. Do not chew or bite your lip, as this makes you look nervous.

Hand gestures

Keep your hands relaxed and visible; do not hide them in your pockets or fiddle with a mobile phone. When making gestures, use your hands boldly to emphasise your words.[14] Make sure you do not fidget with your hands, which will imply that you are nervous.

Finger gestures

15

Pointing is a strong, bold way to emphasise a point but can be seen as a threatening gesture if done too forcefully. The steepling of fingers is a gesture that implies superiority. Don't make exaggerated gestures or you could look foolish.[15]

Shaking hands

A strong bold handshake will express your confidence and strength. Too firm a grip, however, will signify an overpowering personality.

Body contact

You will notice that people in powerful positions avoid any form of body contact, implying that they are beyond the average person's reach.[16] If you want to give an impression of power, then be discerning whom you shake hands with and make sure that any contact is clearly defined. (In our modern democratic culture, our leaders are required to appear humane, approachable and accessible to the person in the street, so you will often see politicians and prime ministers kissing babies and shaking hands with ordinary people.)

Arm gestures

Avoid folding your arms, as this is a negative and defensive gesture and implies displeasure. Make any arm gestures strong, positive and bigger than usual.[17] Also try the opposite and make some minimal gestures. Use your arms to emphasise what you are saying but without gesticulating wildly.[18] For example, instead of nodding your head enthusiastically, try closing your eyes slowly to communicate that you understand; this can often be more powerful.

Leg gestures

Strong leg barriers show a negative and defensive attitude (see pages 87–8). If you cross your legs for comfort, do so in such a way that your feet are pointing towards the person you are talking to.

19

Clothes

Power dressing is one of your strongest allies and can make an instant positive impact. City men and women power-dress to create a strong, forceful, serious impression. Their clothes state that they mean business.[19] Effective power dressing is sharp, precise, neat and invariably makes use of garments of the best quality. Colour experts advocate navy blue as the colour of communication, whereas black can be sombre or stylish and chic.

Shoes should be on the pointed side, and round toes are best avoided altogether. Soft round lines give an impression of comfort, together with a caring, relaxed and easy-going nature – which is not an image you are trying to promote if you are out to power-play.

Exercise: Power dressing

You could do this role-playing exercise with a friend and make it a fun outing.

20

- Consider who, in your opinion, is the most impressive, powerful and inspiring person you know. This could be an actor or pop star, a politician or someone in your local community.
- Consider how they dress in order to present such an impressive image.
- Now get together a similar kind of outfit for yourself.[20] If you do not have the clothes in your wardrobe, ask a friend who has, or head off to a charity shop in an expensive part of town. I always go to Kensington, Chelsea or Mayfair, as the charity shops there often have fantastic, high-quality cast-offs at a fraction of the original price.

- Now dress yourself up in the clothes and try to think yourself into the mind-set of the kind of person who wears them. Remember that you are powerful, confident and high-status at all times. When you are dressed and feeling good about yourself, head off for a drink at the most upmarket place in town – somewhere you would normally not go to. Maintain your high status throughout.
- Now try wearing your outfit to pop into a supermarket or the local pub. Notice how people interact with you.
- Once you are back home again, reflect on how this experience felt for you. Did imagining you were someone else make a difference to your confidence? If so, why? What was it like to be a powerful person? Was it comfortable and enjoyable, or did you feel out of place, awkward or embarrassed? What differences did you notice in your body and the gestures you made?

- If you experienced an increase in confidence, remember how that felt in your body – perhaps you expanded your chest and took in more air, looked the world straight in the eye or had a bounce in your step.[21] Try to repeat these sensations as yourself now. If you did not experience an increase in confidence, see if you can deliberately cultivate some of the positive body language described in this chapter as you go about your business in the next day or two. By practising confident body language you will find that you actually begin to feel more confident in all areas of your life.[22]

Props

23

Keep accessories to a minimum. You want to give an air of strength and efficiency, so think minimalist at all times.[23] Very powerful people have secretaries and PAs, bodyguards and chaperones. They do not answer their own phone calls, so keep your mobile off and out of sight. If you need your phone with you, make sure it is one that will create the right impression.[24] A big out-of-date model will ruin your image in a split second, as will a 'chirpy, chirpy, cheep, cheep' ringtone. Big bulging bags, old briefcases, and plastic carrier bags filled with bits and pieces are definitely out!

Pacing

Power and confidence have a steady pace and, if anything, are a little on the slow side. Moving at a fast pace indicates impatience and nervousness. Power is thoughtful and exacting; it is not rushed. Try holding the attention of an audience for a few moments by making them wait for your important reply.

24

Over-assertiveness

An over-assertive person is someone who wants total control. This sort of person can be dynamic and powerful but is also manipulative and difficult to deal with. Such a person naturally tends to dominate everything and everyone around them. Trying to override them is difficult and leads to confrontation, but harmony can be achieved if you learn to understand what drives them, without feeling a need to try to change them, and at the same time pay special attention to your own needs. A person who is moderately over-assertive may offer you a reassuring feeling of protection and security. On the other hand, a person who is over-assertive in the extreme may be an outright bully, and counteractive measures may have to be taken to deal with them.

An over-assertive person may:

- Have a large personal space zone
- Use large bold gestures such as pointing and thumb displays
- Use minimal facial expressions so as not to give their inner feelings away
- Invade your personal space
- Try to raise themselves above you by towering over you
- Touch you in a way that feels invasive
- Touch your belongings
- Use menacing silence as a weapon to make you feel uneasy
- Look down their nose at you
- Use prolonged eye contact[25]
- Ignore you altogether

25

Responding to an over-assertive person

It is important not to be intimidated by a person who is behaving over-assertively. When confronted with such a person, the most important thing is to keep your own feelings at the forefront of your mind even if your attention is focused on the other person. Maintain your own space and assert your right to your own needs.[26] To pander to the other's every need may seem like an effective, stress-free way to deal with them, but in fact it will only erode your own self-confidence and power. Try the following suggestions:

26

- Remember that you are important; hold your head up and do not be afraid to look the other person in the eye.
- Own your space by planting both feet firmly and squarely on the ground.
- Stand firm and open.
- Place yourself in a higher physical position if possible – stand up if you are sitting.
- If appropriate, use mirroring gestures to suggest that you seek to empathise.
- Use sufficient eye contact (too much is confrontational).

27

I'm better than you: high status and low status

The world we live in today is very much less class-based than that of our grandparents; nevertheless, status – perhaps based less on the class we were born into and more on our material wealth, profession or prominence in the media – remains a powerful social reality. Our social status is often reflected in our overall posture and body language.

Some people are born high-status, others work to achieve it, and yet others just naturally have it.[27] Even if you are not a naturally confident individual, being born into a high-status position will generally give you an air of authority. Being born into the royal family, for instance, will automatically command you respect even if you are not inherently commanding. As a general rule, members of the upper echelons of the class structure, celebrities, heads of companies and the otherwise rich and famous are given respect purely because they are in the public eye and attract public interest. However, being extremely high in status does not automatically make a person an attractive figure – in fact, sometimes the reverse. High social standing incites jealousy and may evoke tribal memories of leadership by violent domination.

28

Tall people tend to be accorded higher status simply because size is considered to be imposing.[28] This size may counteract the effects of a personality more befitting a low-status person. Just think about the language we use to talk about height. We have 'commanding views', 'higher up on the social scale', 'the upper classes and the lower classes', 'high-level jobs' and 'low-life people', to give just a few examples.

It is an interesting fact that actors and TV personalities are often on the short side. Stars such as Dustin Hoffman, Robert de Niro, Sylvester Stallone, Allan Ladd, Frank Sinatra, Barbara Windsor, Bob Hoskins, Jack Dee and Bernie Eccleston, to name but a few, are all surprisingly short in stature. This probably has something to do with the fact that on camera it is hard to judge how tall anyone is. I am sure another factor is that a short person with a big personality and charisma tends to work that extra bit harder to make an impact in the world. On the other side of the coin we have what is sometimes called 'the small man syndrome', referring to those short men who have little going for them in the charm department and exhibit an attitude problem. Such a person is exemplified in the roles often played by Danny de Vito, in which the frustration of being short creates an angry and belligerent attitude towards the world.

29

Aside from our overall social status, which remains more or less constant from day to day (barring a sudden dramatic life change), we all also contain sub-personalities, each with a status of its own. A sub-personality is an embodiment of a role that we play in certain situations and with certain people. It is part of us, but it is not the whole story. For example, at different times I am a wife, a lover, a gardener, an actress, a mother, a writer, a comedian, a horsewoman, a cook, a cleaner, and sometimes a nasty bad-tempered person who is not nice to be around. You may find it useful to write a list of all your sub-personalities. Consider the different status they might have and how that will affect their body language. Most people have a whole range of roles in their lives: traveller;[29] animal lover;[30] entertainer;[31] friend.[32]

30

31

32

33

The status scale

When I am teaching actors, we often do work around status, using a sliding scale from one to ten, one being low-status and ten being high-status. Knowing your character's status level can be an invaluable tool in creating an appropriate body language for them. Each status level has its own characteristic set of expressions, gestures and actions. The ten status levels are as follows:

10 Arrogant, aggressive, over-confident, egomaniacal[33]
9   Ambitious, ruthless, selfish
8   Power-driven, ambitious, successful, possibly unapproachable
7   Charismatic, inspirational
6   Solid, dependable, reliable, with a strong character[34]
5   Well balanced, middle of the road, stable but lacking dynamism
4   Reliable, helpful, caring, tends to be unadventurous[35]
3   Quiet, shy, withdrawn, a pleaser, needy or over-helpful, low self-esteem
2   A loner, unapproachable, a dark character
1   Socially inept, marginalised, no self-confidence, stunted

A typical balanced personality, who can function in society and is accepted by others, might fluctuate between four and seven on the status scale, depending on their mood, the situation and the role they are playing. The majority of people fall within this range. A status below four shows a more shy, withdrawn and private personality, and a status of above seven indicates an outgoing, attention-seeking, dynamic, determined and ambitious person.

A level ten status profile

The following are body language characteristics that you might observe in an individual who scores ten on the status scale above:

36

- Stands tall and erect
- Holds his or her head aloft, possibly tilted backwards, and may give the appearance of looking down their nose at others
- Commands a large area of personal space by distancing him or herself from others and may appear aloof and unapproachable
- May avoid personal eye contact, but if eye contact is made it is piercing[36]
- Makes gestures that are deliberate, defined and exuding power, or minimal and dismissive
- May surround him or herself with other people for protection and to maintain importance

37

This is an extreme and often uncomfortable status position, and a person who holds it may be unpleasant and intimidating to be around.

A level one status profile

These are the characteristics of an individual who scores one on the status scale:

- Appears small, as if wishing to be invisible – shoulders are hunched over, head is held down, hands are clenched tightly together and the whole body is scrunched up, as if in a ball[37]
- Appears nervous and frightened, keeping head averted
- Makes quick and jerky gestures
- Avoids eye contact
- Avoids body contact

38

39

40

Exercise: Status check

This exercise will hone your skills in assessing the status level of the different individuals you come across in real-life situations. It's also interesting and fun!

- Think about your friends and colleagues. Which of them do you really like and admire?[38] Who do you look up to? Who makes you laugh?[39]
- Now look at the scale on page 106 and consider where they fit into it.

When you are around these people, observe how their body language fits (or doesn't fit) their status.

Repeat this exercise with people you dislike.

Then, repeat this exercise again with people you usually choose to ignore.

Status anomalies

We have probably all encountered people in jobs – shop assistant, waiter, bartender – that should make them low in status and thus deferent in their body language but whose behaviour is actually that of someone much higher up the status ladder. Consider for a moment Basil Fawlty in the TV sitcom *Fawlty Towers*. As a hotelier, his job involves behaving in an accommodating and respectful manner towards his clients. In other words, we would expect him to have understated mannerisms, a deferent posture with his head lowered, and a respectful softly spoken voice. What makes this character so compellingly funny, however, is that in fact he behaves in completely the opposite way. He walks tall, holds his head high with his nose in the air, shouts at his customers and is liberal with insults to all and sundry – all characteristics of some high-status people! On TV he might be hilarious but in real life, such a person would be rude and intensely infuriating.[40]

In one of my first jobs as an actress, I had the good fortune to work with one of Britain's most renowned film directors, Ken Loach. He commands a great deal of respect and admiration from the acting profession and has made many wonderful movies, such as *Kes* and *Cathy Come Home*. His work has won him many awards. Yet he is a surprisingly quiet and gentle man, with a compassionate regard for ordinary people. He is softly spoken and shows not the slightest sign of considering himself a person of status.

41

As I sat nervously being made up for our day's shooting, in walked Ken Loach.[41] He said 'hello' politely and asked me how I was. Before I could even reply, the make-up girl asked him in no uncertain terms to get out and leave me alone. As you can imagine, I was rather taken aback. I could not believe she had spoken to him in such a derogatory way. When he had left, she turned to me and said, 'Who was he anyway?' It turned out she was a freelance make-up artist on her first job with this crew. She had obviously never met Ken Loach before, but going by his clothes and his quiet, unassuming manner, she had presumed he was someone of little importance. She later told me she thought he was the caretaker!

42

Mixed status

You might think that a person with a high-status occupation would be a high-status individual. However, a person's job may not give us the whole picture. Most of us will have a slightly different status in different areas of life, and this will be reflected in our body language. In some individuals the discrepancy may be marked. Let's take, for example, the managing director of a successful blue chip company, who has a commandng presence at work.[42] He wakes to the demands of an overpowering wife who once discovered he was having an affair and ever since has assumed the upper hand in the marriage, while he does anything for an easy life and to keep the peace. Let's look at the managing director's body language. He walks around the house with his shoulders hunched. His head is constantly held downwards. He listens to his wife but does not hold eye contact with her.[43] He takes small, quiet steps as if wishing not to be noticed. His body language suggests a status of level three to four.

43

As he closes the front door and sets off for work, the way he thinks and feels changes. He immediately moves up the status ladder, and his body posture reflects this. He stands upright, holds his head high and takes long, confident strides as he walks towards his waiting car. He nods to his chauffeur in greeting as the door is opened for him. Pleasantries are exchanged, during which the chauffeur bows his head, averts his eyes and speaks quietly and politely, signalling his own lower status.

As our man enter his offices, the doorman acknowledges him with a bow of the head, the receptionist says 'good morning' and everyone he passes uses deferent body language. They stand

44

aside to let him walk freely and open doors for him, and his secretary prepares his morning cup of coffee. His status is now at about level eight.

Then the telephone rings. The chief executive officer asks the managing director to come and see him. The CEO commands a status somewhere around level nine and is and quite a formidable character. Our man retains his level eight status but acknowledges the higher status of his peer through his body

language.[44] He waits until a chair is indicated before sitting and then leans forward in his chair, appearing eager to listen. He maintains eye contact, demonstrating confidence while appearing keen and attentive. He holds both hands in front of him, thus creating a barrier between himself and his CEO that gives him a feeling of comfort and support. He speaks when spoken to.[45]

At the end of the day our man returns home to an empty house. His wife is out with friends. He changes out of his formal suit, relaxes and reverts to his private status, which is a comfortable

45

six on the status scale. He slouches into his chair, plays some relaxing music and pours himself a stiff drink. He is pleased with his day and has an air of contentedness. An hour or so later his daughter arrives with his grandson. The grandson is given the highest status of all, as our man rolls on the floor, lifts his grandson into the air, turns into a servant to fetch him drinks and sweets, tells him a story and makes his grandson feel loved and special.

Consider your day and how different people and different situations change your status and thus your body language. Think about situations where it might be useful to you to lower your status. For instance, you might do this deliberately if you were talking to a child, so as not to intimidate him or her. If you need someone on your side or have done something wrong and wish to avoid confrontation, lowering your status can be very effective. If you want something, you may also choose to lower your status, almost kneeling down to ask for it. On the other hand, there are situations where deliberately adopting a higher status can work in your favour, for example if you have to deal with a bully.

Pitching your status

Whenever you are preparing for an important meeting, consider what status level you should pitch yourself at (see page 106). If you want to make a powerful impact, pitch yourself at around the 8 mark.[46]

A word of caution for those of you who already tend to come over as confident – and I include myself in this category.[47] When nervous I am prone to appearing over-confident. This does me no favours at all and has in fact lost me quite a few jobs. If you do fall into this category, then try to contain your nervous energy and make a positive effort to slow yourself down. You want to make a positive impact, not blow everyone out of the water! Remember that power and confidence are about self-respect and a steady, firm belief in your abilities.

Respecting the status of others

In everyday situations, such as at work, we succeed and achieve our objectives in part by pleasing other people. You are unlikely to get promoted in any job unless you are able to communicate effectively, get on well with your colleagues and impress your peers without making yourself appear unpleasantly superior.[48] Accomplishing these glowing attributes requires respect for and sensitivity to the thoughts, desire, wishes and needs of others. Overstepping the mark

49

can ruin your reputation and your career plan in an instant. When you are dealing with a person who commands respect, try the following suggestions:

- Keep your distance and do not impinge upon the other person's space zone.
- Be close enough to remain attentive.[49]
- If possible, position yourself at a lower level. If you cannot help towering over the other person, relax your body and slightly lower your head.
- Keep your eyes generally averted but make eye contact when speaking.

Meeting new people can be a disconcerting experience. Indeed, the stress induced by desiring to make the right impression can often result in the opposite effect. We may appear defensive, spill our drink, say too much, or be too nervous to say anything at all. In such a situation try not to get flustered. Just take a deep breath, remember to be yourself and see if you can put some of your new body language knowledge into practice. You may even find yourself enjoying the experience and soon feel as if you had known them for years.[50]

50

5 I Want to Make an Impression

Every day of our lives we are presented with a range of basic situations that call upon us to present ourselves to the outside world, using appropriate behaviour and body language. The impression we want to make will vary according to which of our many roles – mother, partner, executive, friend and so on – we are playing in the moment. At a job interview or at work, for example, we will probably want to convey an impression of professionalism and efficiency.[1] At a party, on the other hand, we may want to appear bubbly and sociable.[2] In general, however, openness, honesty, trustworthiness and a good sense of humour are attributes that will make a good impression on others and encourage them to get to know you better. Using body language that promotes this image will definitely help you on your way.

Of course, there are other ways to make an impression. Being flamboyant and controversial will get you a lot of attention, but it may not make you a lot of friends in the long term. Creative people often make an impact in society on the strength of their talent alone, while the lack of charm that they sometimes exhibit is excused as 'artistic temperament'. For most of us, however, an amiable personality and open, friendly body language are essential to win popularity.

'Why do we want to make an impression?' you might ask. The simple answer is, we like to be liked and we love to be loved.[3] We desire recognition, and we need to feel accepted and important within our social circle. Being a popular person attracts attention, favours and positive opportunities, making our journey through life easier, more enjoyable and more fruitful. Being able to make a good impression is a self-rewarding activity, which can be satisfying and fulfilling.

4

5

6

First impressions

Of course, as well as making impressions, we also receive impressions about other people. It takes just a few seconds for us to weigh up a person or a situation. When meeting someone for the first time we give them a quick body scan and within a short space of time have come to many conclusions about them, both consciously and unconsciously.[4] We register the basic facts of whether a person is male/female, young/old, short/tall, trendy/old-fashioned and so on. From what we first see we can even hazard a guess as to their financial status, their occupation, if they are married, where they live and their nationality.[5] We also decide whether we like them and – for reasons we may find it difficult to pinpoint – may take an instant dislike to them.[6] We may, on the other hand, be instantly sexually attracted to them, in which case our body language will change accordingly – our posture will alter, our speech rhythms will change and we may use seductive patterns of eye contact.

I feel it is true to say that women tend to use much wider criteria than men when assessing a person and generally register far more information. Is this because by nature we are a more inquisitive creature than the male of our species or is it to do with some natural basic instinct? I feel that as mothers and protectors of our young we have evolved the ability to make rapid and accurate assessments of any given situation. Our instinctive drive is to protect our children, and so we are on alert for any potential danger. In my observation, women who have reared children are often more perceptive and more readily able to read non-verbal forms of communication – probably because during the first few years of a child's life the majority of its communication is non-verbal.

When we need to impress

You may be the sort of person who wants to impress everybody all of the time, but this is a very exhausting way to live. There are, however, moments in all of our lives when we feel the need to excel ourselves for a special occasion or important situation. Examples include:

- At an important meeting
- Making a speech
- Performing on stage
- At an interview
- Networking
- Meeting future in-laws
- In the public eye
- In politics

The following are some pointers for making the very best of yourself in any situation.

Head up

Lifting your head up will not only give an impression of confidence in a one-to-one situation, but will also enable you to project your voice if you are addressing an audience.[7] In this situation, make sure you speak to the people at the back of the room as well as those in the front row.

Eye contact

Make eye contact with every person you are speaking to.[8] If you are giving a speech or addressing a large group, make eye contact with as many people as possible, as you do so, speaking to them as if individually, each in turn. Once you have one person's attention, move on to another in a different location and avoid going back to the same person too frequently. The more people you maintain eye contact with, the greater the impact.[9]

Hand gestures

Use your hands to emphasise your words. A useful hand gesture is the appeal, showing the palms of your hands to express honesty and inform whoever you are speaking to that you have nothing to hide.[10] This gesture is an inviting one, asking the other person to participate and involving them. If you are giving a talk that involves showing diagrams or slides, use a baton or thin stick to point to your designated object. This creates a point of focus and directs your audience directly to what you want them to see. It is also much more dramatic than pointing with a finger.

Observe

Observe the body language of the person or people you are speaking to. Are they looking at you, nodding in agreement, with attentive eyes? Or are they looking bored, fidgety and falling asleep?[11] If you have lost their attention, do something to win it back. Be bold, ask them a question, take your jacket off, change the subject, tell them a joke ... anything that is appropriate to the situation. Notice if anyone you are speaking to is sitting with their arms and legs crossed. This is a defensive gesture and they are likely to be in disagreement with you. If they are leaning back with hands clasped behind their head, not only do they not agree with you but they think they know better. Do not let this put you off; it is a great opportunity that you should grasp. Try picking them out and telling them that you can see they disagree with you. Ask them why, and what they would suggest instead. If you can involve them and get them back into the action, it will have a domino effect upon everyone else. If you are speaking to a group, you can then invite questions; people will now be eager to join in and will contribute to the ensuing discussion in a lively manner – and they are likely to remember your speech for a long time.

Passion

Passion is an instinctive emotion that comes straight from the heart. When we are speaking passionately, we don't care about what others think of us. We appear alive, energised. Our eyes are wide open, focused and direct, signalling that we want what we say to be heard and understood. Passion can also be fuelled by rage, in which case it is usually accompanied by defiant hand gestures such as pointing and beating in rhythm with the voice. If you are giving a speech, deliver it with as much passion as you can muster.[12] Passion is enthralling, and even if your audience do not agree with you, they will be captivated by your fire.

Dress to impress

Dress smartly – otherwise people will be focused on your tatty outfit. If necessary, hire clothes that are appropriate for the situation.[13]

At an interview

Going for interview is a stressful and nerve-wracking experience for most people. Fortunately for most of us, it does not happen too frequently within our working lifetime. For actors, however, auditions are a regular occurrence – and no less intimidating for that, believe me. The constant cycle of self-esteem building and repeated rejection can be a weighty burden to carry day in, day out. In time and with luck one develops a sense of optimistic fatalism – 'If it's meant to be and it's right for you, you'll get the job.'

Some great words of wisdom were given to me many years ago. When confronted with yet another interview, I bring them to mind, just before I step in front of the firing squad. The people interviewing you are sitting there in the expectation that the right person is about to walk through that door.[14] They are anticipating the best and are fervently hoping that that person is you.

15

Present yourself at your very best – be fresh, alert and alive. Prepare yourself – do your homework. Practise in front of a mirror.[15] If you perform as well as you possibly can, then you have fulfilled your obligation 100 per cent. The rest is up to fate. Remember, even if you do not get the job, the meeting and the contact you have made are still important. If you have made a good impression, you may be remembered for a position later on, or your name may be suggested to someone else.

Interview body language

Sitting in isolation in front of an interview panel can be intimidating, but there is a reason for this seating arrangement. It enables the panel to have a full view of you and your body language, so make sure you pay as much attention to what your body is communicating as to what you say verbally.

- Sit upright and lean slightly forwards. Leaning forwards shows your interest and enthusiasm. Leaning backwards, on the other hand, can appear aloof and judgemental.
- Keep your body posture open. If you have to cross your legs, then point your foot towards the main speaker, otherwise you are creating a defensive barrier. Do not fold your arms. Don't slouch or fidget.[16]
- Keep your body movements to a minimum or you will give the impression of being nervous and uncomfortable.
- Maintain eye contact with the person who is speaking to you primarily, but also be sure to make some eye contact with everyone else in the room when you speak.
- Remember to breathe easily and to smile.

16

Networking

'Networking' describes the various activities we perform to make connections with others, and to share, circulate and propagate information. When networking we may therefore use body language that we might not ordinarily adopt on meeting a stranger. For example, we may stand closer than we generally would to someone we do not know, because we want to give the impression of being their friend. Open and friendly body language is called for here, and this can take some getting used to if you are a naturally retiring type of person.[17] If you feel uncomfortable in a room full of virtual strangers, then pace yourself and take one step at a time.

- Do not be afraid to approach a total stranger.
- Introduce yourself and shake hands if appropriate.
- Ask questions, for example about the other person's occupation. When they are responding, tilt your head slightly to one side to show that you are interested and listening to what they are saying.[18]
- Nod your head to encourage the other person to speak.
- If you are feeling brave, try reaching out and gently touching their arm. This is easier to do when something humorous has been said.
- Try telling them something they may find of particular interest. Approach them by tilting your head towards their eye and placing a hand on their shoulder – this is a gesture of closeness and friendship. Lower your voice as you speak.[19]
- Do not overstay your welcome and attempt to make contact as you leave – perhaps by shaking hands or just with a nod and a smile.

Body language to make a social impression

If you want to create a good impression in a social situation, a great ploy – and one that I use often – is to imagine that the gathering is being held purely for your own benefit. This notion helps to dispel any feelings of low self-esteem. The pressure eases, and I can relax and enjoy myself rather than being on edge all the time.[20] I find it easier to keep a smile on my face and have a laugh and a joke. I am able to mingle with everyone and feel happy to reach out and touch people. Try this for yourself. You will find that the gathering becomes a wonderful experience. You will be eager to meet people, more proactive in introducing yourself and more inclined to take the initiative with people.

Personal space

The desire to make an impression goes hand in hand with wanting to get closer to a person or a group of people, which means you not only need to be approachable yourself but you also need to make a direct effort to approach them. At first, aim for a social distance – approximately at arm's length; then, when conversation has become free-flowing and you sense you have made a connection, try moving slightly closer.[21] If this feels comfortable to you and if your new position is accepted by the other person, you will know you have made positive inroads. Be sensitive to their personal space at all times, as you want to make an good impression, not become an unwanted nuisance.

Once you are satisfied you have made the desired impact, a good rule of thumb is to back off a little. Take a small step backwards and see if they move in towards you to make the space personal once again. If they do, you know you have been successful. Don't over-expose the other party to your presence. One ploy might be to make your excuses, move away for a while and return later, now allowing them to make overtures to you. Leave them intrigued and wanting more.

Posture

Make sure your body is relaxed but energised and if anything leaning slightly forwards. This position shows you are alert and gives the air of somebody enthusiastic and interested.

A casual and sociable position to place yourself in is slightly at an angle to another person.[22] This leaves space for a third party to join you and allows both parties to casually observe the rest of the gathering while taking note of any other action. Standing face to face blocks other people from joining you and is also an indication that what you are discussing is private.

Head positions

Lean your head slightly forward to indicate your interest and nod occasionally to show that you understand and are absorbing what is being said. When listening intently, we also tend to lean the head to one side.[24]

Facial expressions

React to what is being said. A blank expressionless face indicates a lack of interest. Smile and laugh to encourage other people to talk.[23]

Eye signals

Maintain direct eye contact when listening, and make sure you do genuinely listen, no matter how bored you are by what the person is saying. Do not be distracted by someone or something more interesting.

If you have not yet been introduced to the person with whom you would like to make an association, smile at them from a distance, make eye contact, then look away. When you do get to meet, both of you will feel much more at ease with each other.

25

Mouth expressions

Try to keep a relaxed mouth and smile when appropriate. A smile makes you seem more friendly and approachable.[25]

Hand gestures

Open hand gestures indicate honesty and also help you appear more accessible.[26] Avoid barriers of all kinds, as these have the effect of keeping others at bay. Make sure your hands are relaxed and hold on to a drink if you feel the need of a prop.

26

Touching

Touching in social situations is perfectly acceptable, but it needs to be sensitive and appropriate. Be aware of where you touch another person, especially if you do not know them too well. The arm, shoulder or hands are safe, non-taboo areas. A friendly touch can accompany such questions and statements as, 'Can I get you a drink?', 'Do you have any children?' 'I'm glad we had the chance to talk' and 'You are so funny!'. Touching is an intimate gesture and suggests that you have bonded. Be careful not to overdo it, though, or you will be regarded as being intrusive. Women in particular hate invasively touchy men.

27

Body contact

With people you know, make a fuss and hug and kiss them. Go on, be flamboyant and delighted to see them! Genuine warmth and affection is the most attractive characteristic that anyone can possess and certainly makes the deepest impression of all.[27] We all need attention and we all desperately need to be loved. Not only does spreading a bit of joy have a positive effect on everyone you meet, it is also a valuable tonic for your own soul.

Arm gestures

I love showy people and, boy oh boy, do big arm gestures make an impression. At a party or social event, make an entrance in the most creative way possible. Fling your arms wide open and exclaim a fond hello to all your friends. This will certainly have people looking at you and paying you plenty of attention. With people you know, throw your arms open and give them a big hug.[28] If someone you do not know is staring at you wondering what on earth you are doing, go on, be bold, give them a big hug too!

A friend of mine was having his 40th birthday party and I wanted to do something special. I dressed as a life-sized birthday card. My arms held the large card closed, and as I opened my arms, the card, which was me, sang 'Happy Birthday'. I certainly made an entrance, and he had the biggest and most unique birthday card.

Leg gestures

Whether you are standing or sitting, point your feet towards the person of your interest. Avoid using barrier leg positions (see pages 87–8).

Clothes

If the event you are attending is formal or is connected with your professional life, certain dress codes will be in force and are best adhered to. However, you can still make subtle alterations and adjustments to make a statement, such as a sharp haircut or an unusual accessory that will cause interest without being provocative. If the event is a purely a social situation, then dare to be as extreme and eye-catching as you possibly can.[29] Have fun with how you look.

Props

In the acting world, celebrities will do absolutely anything to make the biggest impact of all. I have seen the most amazing – and startling – of exhibitions: limos, bodyguards, helicopters, jumping out of life-sized cakes, see-through

30

clothes and even topless female bodyguards, weird outfits, impersonations.[30] The list is endless, and I have been amused and delighted by many an impressive gesture. If you can afford it, why not? It is all harmless fun. Just bear in mind, however, the kind of impression you want to make. If you are a small-town solicitor whose aim is to attract an upmarket clientele, arriving at a bash in a helicopter with topless female bodyguards is probably not going to impress.

Body mirroring

31

Mirroring happens naturally when you are close to someone but you can also use it to your advantage.[33] A good way to demonstrate affinity with another person is to mirror their actions and gestures. For example, when they lift their glass and take a drink, do likewise.[32] Observe the way they are holding their body and adopt a similar posture. Make sure your mirroring is not blatantly obvious and delay a second or two before you make your move.

Of course, if the other person is using barrier signals – crossd arms or legs, lack of eye contact – it is not wise to mirror them![31] If their body posture appears negative, defensive and closed down, try asking them a question about themselves or their work and be interested in their reply. This may help them feel more relaxed, and with any luck they will change their posture to a more positive one. As and when they do, you can begin to mirror them.

32

33

Timing

Try to take the initiative, as this will get you noticed. Take the lead, be positive and instigate actions.

Exercise: Brush up your social body language

- Talk to a stranger and make them the most interesting person in the room.[34] Discover what makes them so interesting. During your conversation try to make some appropriate tactile contact, such as touching their arm, hand or wrist, or giving them a gentle pat on the back.
- Talk to someone you would normally instinctively ignore. Notice what it is about them and their body language that usually makes you want to back off. Make a genuine effort to get to know them. Try introducing yourself with a nod of the head or a smile – or a formal handshake if this is more appropriate to the situation. Try to open the conversation with a compliment or a friendly question while maintaining eye contact. Bear in mind that your natural instinct will be defensive, so make sure you do not fold your arms or adopt a closed posture. Does your opinion of this person change during the conversation? Are they far more interesting than they first appeared?
- Approach someone you find sexually attractive and talk to them.[35] Do you still find them attractive after you have got to know them a little more or does your opinion change? When you've done it once, it will be easier the second time – and practice makes perfect!

When someone is trying to impress you

When someone makes an effort to impress you personally, you become the focus of their attention. This experience can be flattering, disconcerting or even disturbing, depending on the circumstances.

When a person tries to impress you with their power and affluence, they are using a manipulative ploy – and it often works because these are the very things many of us

strive for in life ourselves. The film *Indecent Proposal* is a great example of this situation. Robert Redford entices Demi Moore away from her husband for $1 million. She agrees to sleep with him for the money so that she and her husband can have a better life. The trappings of the rich and powerful prove far too tempting for her, however, and as she consents to his advances, slowly but surely her marriage begins to crumble.

Often when a person tries to impress you, they go out of their way to please you. This could be by being overly friendly, offering to accommodate your wishes even at inconvenience to themselves, and generally making sure you are more than comfortable and have everything you need. If they want to get to know you better, they may engage you in conversation, ask questions and possibly offer to see you again. A person who impinges too closely and eagerly on your private space zone and personal life can feel intimidating and possibly threatening.[36] Any attempt to invade your space should alert your suspicions and make you cautious about allowing this relationship to develop.[37]

On the other hand, a person who is attentive, remembers your name, makes you feel comfortable and appears genuinely interested in you, may be a connection worth nurturing.

Notice how you react to their interest. Do you smile? Does your body become more relaxed? Do you find yourself looking them directly in the eye. If they have made tactile contact, notice where they touched you and how you felt about that.

So you see, you don't necessarily require bucket-loads of money or a fast car to impress; the art of good body language will take you a long way. Try a few of the tips in this chapter and see for yourself.

6 Do You Fancy Me?

We begin to learn about intimate relationships as babes in arms. The bond we establish with our parents will set many of the patterns for our love relationships in adult life. As children we continue to thrive and develop in response to being held, caressed, touched, kissed and stroked. As we venture into adolescence and beyond, the parental bond begins to ebb and we start to discover our own sexuality and identity. Our need for physical reassurance from our parents diminishes, and we start to look to boyfriends and girlfriends to meet our emotional needs.

To attract a mate we use a vast array of display signals and courtship gestures, many of them completely unconscious. Women use far more courtship signals than men and are also far better at reading them. Male or female, however, we are sexual beings and enjoy expressing our sexuality not only to find a life partner and procreate our species but also for our own pleasure and enjoyment. Most of us at some time innocently play at flirting with friends, colleagues and even strangers.[1] This is harmless and fun and, if we are already in a committed relationship, does not mean that we are likely to stray.[2] It is very natural to continue to find other people attractive even though we have a life partner; it is also natural to like being looked at, admired and considered sexy. This reinforces our attractiveness and is important for our self-esteem and morale.

It is important to be fluent in body language in order both to understand what signals we are sending out and to be able to decode the responses.[3] Many years ago I was so

4

convinced that a particular gorgeous guy was madly in love me that I boldly made a move and told him how I felt about him. If only I had known then what I know now about the subtleties of body language I would have saved myself the excruciating embarrassment of throwing myself at a gay man who was happily ensconced in a long-term, loving relationship … Ah well!

How to tell when someone fancies you

Okay, girls, so you walk into a room and all the guys look at you. Terrific. That is exactly the impact a girl wants to make. When women dress alluringly, provocatively and sexily, it is generally not because they want to sleep with every guy in town but because they love the attention, adore being admired and like to be seen as sexy.[4] It works in reverse too, of course. A man knows how to look sexy in order to draw admiring glances.[5] These days, sexy is good. It's what sells. It makes the world go round.

5

A man walking into a room with a beautiful sexy woman by his side has the most sought-after of accessories. He will be the envy of all his friends and colleagues.[6] Vicariously, he, too, is making the impact he desires. Some men, however, find having a beautiful woman by their side difficult to deal with, feeling constantly anxious about losing her to someone else. If your partner is prone to this kind of jealousy, then he is battling with his own insecurities. Be sensitive to them but do not lose your own identity in appeasing his irrational fears.

While I was working for the BBC recently, one of my male colleagues confessed to being besotted with one of the female presenters. He was clearly admiring her from afar, and I suggested he make a play for her. However, he looked horrified. 'I can't,' he said. 'I just go to pieces when she talks to me and turn into a blithering idiot.' Poor guy. I am sure we have all experienced this form of attraction. Yet this man was impressively confident and self-assured – except when he was in the company of the presenter. He worshipped her, but he was never going to find out if there was a possibility of a relationship between them unless he could get a little

6

closer to her. Just a smile in her direction, even from the other side of the studio, would have been a great start.

There are several overt pieces of body language that clearly signal attraction. Look out for these immediate and generally subconscious actions and gestures if you are meeting someone for the first time.

Suck and tuck

'Suck and tuck' is a great phrase that I picked up in the US. I was taking in the sun by my hotel swimming pool in Los Angeles, a city full of beautiful young hopefuls, when a Hollywood film mogul walked by. A young girl who was sitting with a group of friends whispered to the others, 'Suck and tuck, girls,' upon which the whole bevvy of beauties pushed their finely sculpted bosoms out as far as possible while at the same time tucking in their tummies, as with beaming white smiles they posed for the big shot parading by. He swelled with pride and instinctively adjusted himself to a greater height, pushed out his chest (not so sculpted, I might add) and tightly held in his protruding paunch. He smiled to his colleague as though this happened to him all the time, which no doubt it did.

7

In the case of the girls, the suck and tuck was done quite deliberately and cynically, but it is in fact also an instinctive reaction – on the part of both men and women – to the sight of someone we fancy so that we display our bodies to their best advantage.[7]

Hip sway

When a woman walks past a man or a group of men she finds attractive, she will instinctively tend to sway her hips. I am extremely aware of doing this myself and have consciously tried to stop doing it, but I find it virtually impossible.[8]

8

9

Preening

When a man sees someone he is attracted to, if he is standing he will draw himself up to his full height and will often open his legs wider, as if to display his genital area. He appears to be preening himself just as a bird does (a male bird will stand back, ruffle its feathers and clean them on meeting a female). He may check his clothes, slick back his hair and dust himself down as if wanting to present himself at his best.[9]

Hair

A woman's hair is considered, by its very nature, to be a sign of sexuality. Long flowing hair is seen as feminine and alluring. Tousled across the face, it conveys a sexy, just-rolled-out-of-bed impression. Short, boyish hair implies a fun, spirited and impish nature. Rigid styles and excessive grooming suggest that a woman may be fussy, particular and even somewhat frigid.

10

Whether their hair is long or short, women often react to an attractive person by using a head toss gesture, as if they are tossing their hair away from their face.[10] This allows a better look at the face and draws attention in the woman's direction. Fiddling with the hair is also very common. If long, it can be played with sensually by sucking and drawing the ends out of the mouth in a sexually suggestive fashion.

Men also signal attraction by touching their hair, but they tend to smooth or comb it with their fingers.

Head gestures

A common gesture used by women is the sideways 'peek-a-boo' glance.[11] This is a quick sensual look, often with lowered eyelids, and then a rapid turn away. This establishes contact and invites the admirer to continue looking. Another female gesture is the lowering of the head with a slow eye close. This is an enticing look and implies a submissive nature. (If the head is held high, it implies a woman who likes to take a more dominant role.)

11

Blushing

Both men and women may blush in response to the attention of an admirer – a reaction that is often experienced as embarrassing. The face reddens as heat rises upwards from the lower neck region, and with some people the reddening can also affect the neck and chest.[12] Blushing is most often a problem during adolescence and is an automatic reaction to embarrassment. It is difficult – if not impossible – to stop, but as we gain in confidence and maturity, it tends to disappear of its own accord.

Eye signals

In the game of sexual courtship many gestures are tantalising in intent and are often displayed from a distance in order to establish eye contact. Women and many gay men seem to have an uncanny ability to sense when they are being observed by an admirer and after establishing initial eye contact will often gesture in a seductive and provocative manner knowing full well they are being watched.[13] Once the couple get closer, eye contact is maintained and the courtship dance will continue mostly face to face. Men tend to hold strong eye contact, while a woman will smile in a submissive manner, implying that she is flattered and acknowledging the attention from her admirer.

Holding eye contact for just a moment longer than normal suggests an attraction; longer than that suggests a desire for intimacy. If the gaze lowers from the eyes to the lips and the upper neck, this clearly indicates sexual attraction.[14] Men's eyes are naturally drawn to a woman's breasts and bottom.[15] When sexually attracted, women, too, will admire a man's buttocks, looking for firmness and muscle power, and often cannot resist stealing a look at the genital region.

16

Dilated pupils suggest immediate sexual interest and are described as bedroom eyes. When we turn down the lights and use candles to encourage a romantic atmosphere, the dimness naturally dilates the pupils, thus enhancing the impression of mutual attraction. The likes of Robert Redford, Paul Newman (in the photograph), and Marlon Brando have bright blue piercing eyes in which dilation of the pupils is clearly visible, making them irresistible to women.[16] (For more on dilated pupils see pages 49–50.)

Mouth expressions

Women will moisten their mouths and hold their lips slightly open in an alluring sexual manner.[17] This look is suggestive of the moistened vagina and suggests readiness for penetration and sexual intercourse. Rubbing the tongue across the lips to moisten them suggests the same thing. (For more information, see page 26.)

17

Hand gestures

The eye will be drawn to wherever the hand is placed on the body or where it directs the eye.[18] The thigh, the shoulder and the base of the throat are all sensual areas in a woman; however, gently rubbing any area of the skin can be a seductive gesture. The delicate underside of the wrist is highly erotic and is often exposed when smoking or taking a drink.

A woman will often place her hand on her hips in order to draw attention to her childbearing capacity. Men, too, will often place their hands on their hips. This makes them appear larger than they really are and gives them confidence as a result. Men also often touch their genitals in an absentminded way, as if checking to see if they are still there! This gesture expresses a desire for reassurance. Holding the genitals in a more forceful way is a clear display of manhood and its needs. (It can also be a sign to another man that something is a 'ball ache'.)

18

Finger gestures

A woman places her fingers in her mouth to suggest intercourse. Slowly placing food in the mouth and consuming it is also very erotic.[19] For a man, using the aggressive thumbs-in-the-belt gesture (see page 27) draws the eye line to the 'ready for action' genital area. (This gesture is also occasionally used by women.)

19

Touching

Sensual touching is done by both men and women and is a stage in the foreplay of love-making. Pinching and child's play are often performed to suggest the desire for more intimacy.[20] People who are sexually attracted will find any way to make physical contact with the object of their desire. Lovers will indulge in constant bodily contact, holding hands, putting their arms around each other or kissing in public. They will talk to friends with arms wrapped around each other, happily intertwined – physically and emotionally – for all the world to see.

20

On the dance floor total strangers can within a few moments be unashamedly gyrating their hips together or in a tight genitalia-touching embrace if a slow smoochie record is played.[21] The dance floor is a place to celebrate your sexuality, where the normal rules of propriety do not altogether apply and you can release all that pent-up sexual energy with gusto.

21

22

Thighs

Women tend to sit or stand with their legs wider apart when an attractive man is around, subconsciously drawing attention to their genital area (see page 24). If wearing a skirt, a woman may cross her legs slowly, in so doing not only exposing her thighs but also offering a tantalising glimpse of what is beyond. Women will often run their hands over their thighs to draw attention there; when crossing their legs they may do so with a little more pressure than normal in order to highlight the muscle tone of their thighs.

23

Knees and toes

Knee-pointing is a female posture in which a seated woman tucks one leg under the other, while the upper knee points towards the object of her sexual interest.[22] In this position the genital area is open and the observer's eye is naturally drawn to the thigh area.

Toe-pointing is an easy gesture to spot when you first start observing body language. When standing, both men and women will point their feet towards a person they are attracted to. This gesture can also be observed in people who are sitting, as long as both feet are on the floor.

An erotic foot gesture is the toe-dangling shoe.[23] This is indicative of the thrusting action of the penis during intercourse. It may look innocent enough, but it certainly gives the game away!

24

A very good friend of mine was married to a man who was an out-and-out womaniser. He systematically compromised each of her friends in turn, in the hope of extramarital sexual encounters. This came to light one evening when a group of us met together for supper and for some reason my friend was unable to join us. The topic of conversation eventually got round to her husband. It emerged that he had tried it on with all of us. We discovered he always made the first move when he and his wife were invited to dinner. Seated at the dinner table, he would rub his foot up and down another female guest's leg, knowing full well that she would not say anything while his wife was innocently sitting there.[24] As good friends, we told his wife. Thankfully, he is no longer around.

Clothes

Clothes project an image, and if a man or woman goes out with the intention of finding a partner they will dress accordingly. Sexy clothes do not, however, mean that a person is sexually available to all and sundry.

Props

25

Many objects can be toyed with in a sexually suggestive fashion. Think of how pole dancers and lap dancers brazenly gyrate around customised poles and improvise around other cylindrical objects.[25] Among those of us who don't make our living this way, the cigarette is often used as a phallic symbol, seductively placed in the mouth and caressed by the lips before inhaling.[26] In the early days of movie-making it was not permissible to show sex scenes, so cigarette smoking was used as a visual way of suggesting that a couple had made love. Smoking a cigarette and letting the smoke linger between pursed open lips is another extremely seductive gesture used frequently in the era of black-and-white movies.

26

Watch out for the sensual rubbing up and down of the stem of a wine glass done by women in a most absent-minded way but most explicit in intention.[27] You will often see women sliding their hands up and down the stem of their wine glass. This is an extremely erotic gesture and one that is a positive signal to any opportunist male.

Mirror imaging

27

When two people are attracted to one another (or simply like each other), they will begin the harmonising body dance of mirror imaging. When one person makes a movement, the other will swiftly copy it – for example, if one person shifts in their seat, so will the other; if one takes a drink, shortly afterwards the other will too. The actions are not done either consciously or simultaneously but follow one another after the briefest of pauses.

If any form of conflict occurs, mirror imaging will halt until harmony is restored. Imagine, for example, that a couple are having a simple discussion over a cup of coffee.

28

They are relaxed and are mirror-imaging while in conversation.[28] Suddenly an unfamiliar person joins them. They stop mirror-imaging, fold their arms to form a defensive barrier and shift in their chairs, turning their bodies and faces away. A similar change in body language might be observable if, say, one of the couple raises a contentious topic.

Into your personal space

Our personal space is an intimate zone which we do not expect those other than family, lovers and close friends to enter without being invited.[29] An obvious way of doing this is by opening our arms wide – a physical invitation to a hug. Subtler gestures may include a look of appeal, such as fluttering the eyelashes, beckoning with the hands and smiling encouragingly. (See also Chapter 3.)

29

How to respond to another person's advances

If you are enjoying the other person's attention, then you have plenty of ammunition here to encourage the relationship.[30] On the other hand, if you don't want to take things any further, try a knowing smile in acknowledgement, followed by turning away and carrying on with what you were doing. If you are married, you could flash your wedding ring. Better still, if you have a partner and they are close at hand, make clear and definite body contact with them. A cuddle or a kiss will certainly deter any further advances. If you do not have a partner, you could always try borrowing a friend for a few moments (just make sure you explain what you are doing first!).

30

If you want to stop another's advances completely, hold strong eye contact, then cut it off abruptly. A sharp turning away of the head should do it, or turn your back.[31] Disconnecting from an unwanted admirer can be uncomfortable, but if you don't do it, you can get yourself into all sorts of complications. Men in particular need to have lack of interest clearly indicated, as they often misread the signals. Being polite and friendly will be taken as a sign that you are interested and will only encourage them.

31

A girlfriend of mine recently came to stay for the weekend, along with her partner. She is a confident American woman, very bubbly and outgoing, and has flaming red hair. We went along to our village pub for a Sunday lunchtime drink. A few of the local farmers were around us, and my friend was soon the centre of attention. She was having fun and enjoying the repartee when one of the guys overstepped the mark. The next moment he was lying on the floor as she bellowed, 'I wouldn't try that one again!' He explained later that he was so instantly enamoured that he could not resist caressing her ample breasts, even though his partner was standing there with him!

32

While there's no need to throw your admirer on the floor, when shunning unwanted advances you do need to be firm and decisive. Avoid eye contact, turn away and ignore them.[32] If the other person will still not leave you alone, try moving away from them or making some discouraging gesture such as throwing your arms in the air or pushing them forcefully away. They may not like it but at least they will get the message.

Some words of caution

Sexual attraction is often immediate, and the way we react with our body language is automatic and, in some respects, almost impossible to control. Being attracted to someone is a physical experience and is not falling in love, although the feeling may progress into love if a relationship is established. Being sexually attracted to someone is natural and makes us feel vibrantly alive and in the moment.[33] We can enjoy the attention and the experience without acting upon it. Maturity, personal ethics and just basic common sense tell us not to act our attraction out shamelessly, in a way that would be destructive to ongoing relationships.

I recall once reading some words of wisdom by Doris Stokes, a renowned medium. She said that when a person experiences the heady heights of sexual attraction accompanied by uncontrollable feelings of passion, they should regard this as an illness and very dangerous. In fact so dangerous are these feelings that the people involved should walk away and vow never to see each other again, even if one of them has to leave the country! The words made me laugh but they contain a grain of truth. When we think we are in love, the logical brain has a tendency to switch off. It would seem that we have to experience the pain of our mistakes before we have the wisdom to know better, but there's no need to go on repeating them.

33

Exercise: Sexual reactions

This exercise will enable you to become more aware of how you express your sexuality in body language and how others respond.

34

- Next time you are in a social or public place take notice of anyone looking at you.[34]
- Now become aware of your own body language. Did it invite this attention? Is it responding?
- Consider how you would like to respond. Use the relevant body language as described in this chapter.
- Pay attention to the other person's reaction. Is it the desired one?

Exercise: Getting to know you

If you are a shy person and find making contact difficult, try this exercise.

35

- Next time your attention is drawn to someone you would like to know better, establish solid eye contact and then try introducing yourself – or ask another person to introduce you.[35]
- Watch out for any positive body signalling, such as toe pointing, preening or intimate eye gazes. Try lowering your gaze to the other person's lip area and see if they respond by doing likewise. (Make sure your gesture is subtle.)

This is an area where practice will make you more adept at using body language, and it will also give you a lot of confidence in your own powers of attraction.

7 I Care About You

Caring and being cared for are part of what it is to be human. At one time or another most of us will be carers – whether we are looking after a child or an elderly relative, visiting a friend in hospital or working in a professional caring role such as nursing or social work.

There will also be times when we are at the other end of the equation. We have all been children and needed parental care, and we will all require support in old age. Many of us will spend a period in hospital and almost all of us will have benefited from a teacher at some stage in our lives.

Caring, of course, has its own repertoire of body language, which is what we will be discussing in this chapter. Some of the situations in which you might expect to observe or use it (aside from those mentioned above) include:

- When a person is crying[1]
- When a person is in need of comfort or encouragement[2]
- With someone you love
- When a person is afraid[3]
- When a friend is in shock or distress
- When a person is ill

4

Using the body to show you care

Comfort and reassurance are important to everyone from childhood to old age.[4] Take me, for example. I am terrified of dentists. Once inside the surgery I revert to the quivering fear of an infant. I have to hold the dental nurse's hand during treatment and I constantly ask if everything is going to be all right. It is the same every visit, and without the comfort and reassurance of my dentist and the nurses I would never go back for treatment.

5

If you see that another person is in need of comfort and you want to help, try using some of the following body language. Imagine that frightened little child who resides in us all. Put aside the inhibitions of the adult and try to reach the quivering, terrified child within.[5]

Personal space

When offering comfort and support, it is okay to enter another's personal space zone. Be sensitive to their reaction, however. Make your movements slow but firm, so that they are calming and do not appear threatening.[6] It is important to take control and to make decisions, as a person who is deeply distressed is unlikely to be able to do so for themselves.

6

Posture

Lower your body to the other person's level or as close as you can get to it.[9] It is intimidating to have someone towering above you. Positioning your body even lower than theirs can also be useful, as it will make them feel special and important.[10] This is a good position to adopt when talking to a child. Lean towards the other person, as this declares your interest and undivided attention.

Head positions

Nodding your head as the other person is speaking will encourage them to talk and will reassure them that you are interested.[7] Maintaining eye contact will encourage them further.

    If you need to be the person in control, then keep your head upright. If you are being sympathetic, you may wish to tilt your head sideways. This will show that you are listening and absorbing what is being said.

Facial expressions

A gentle smile is always reassuring. Keep your mouth relaxed and try to show no signs of tension, as these will be relayed to the other person.[8] If the person you are dealing with is frightened, then acknowledge what they are saying but do not react to their panic. Maintain a firm compassionate expression. This should allay their fears.

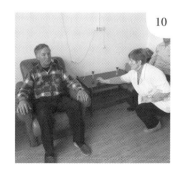

11

Eye signals

If you are ministering to someone who is in shock, maintain eye contact as you talk to them. With someone who is troubled, try looking them in the eye and asking them how they are. This will encourage them to open up and talk to you.

Hand gestures

A solid hand on the other person's wrist or arm is reassuring, particularly if they are in shock. Patting the arm or shoulder is comforting.[11] Stroking the back or arm has a calming effect and conveys your concern. We use this kind of stroking and patting when holding babies and children.

Approaching a person with open hands will demonstrate your honesty and is helpful when you want to establish trust and a sense of safety.

If you need to encourage someone to approach you, use the familiar 'come here' gesture of holding your hands out and rhythmically curling your fingers towards yourself.[12]

12

Finger gestures

13

Tracing a person's face with your finger is an intimate loving gesture and can be used with people you know well and also with children.[13] It is, of course, not advisable to do this to a stranger, as it could be construed as sexual in intent.

(Tickling, although used to make someone laugh, is actually an aggressive gesture with sexual implications.)

Touching

Touch is very comforting. If a person is in a state of fear or panic, maintain firm physical contact with them. Once their fear has subsided, maintain a lighter hold. A hand placed on their wrist or hand in a moderate to firm way will convey a sense of emotional strength that is reassuring. A hand on the face is comforting.[16] People often gain comfort from touching their own face.[14] If a person is in severe distress or grief, a firm supportive body hug can also be reassuring, as can a shoulder to cry on. They may also find it comforting to hug themselves or keep their arms closed.

Arm gestures

Refrain from using defensive arm barrier gestures.[17] Placing one arm around a child or person in need of care is a supportive gesture. If a person is in serious distress, try hugging them and slowly rocking them to and fro, just as you would to soothe a child. This will usually calm the person in a few moments. When you feel the tension is passing, slowly release your hold.

Leg gestures

Refrain, too, from using defensive leg barriers. Point your legs and feet towards the person who needs your attention.

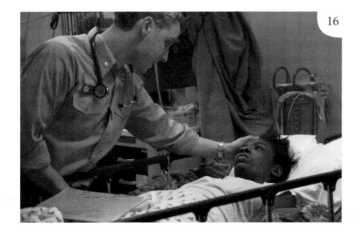

Exercise: reach out and touch somebody

Caring for someone with genuine love, warmth and compassion naturally manifests itself in physical form, such as tender touching, stroking, hugging, smiling and so on. We sometimes forget to show those closest to us that we care; they probably know that we do, but everyone benefits from being reminded now and again. This exercise will help you practise showing love through body language.

- Use body language to thank someone who loves you unconditionally. Stand in front of them, reach out and touch them. Make firm eye contact, smile and tell them how much you appreciate having them in your life.[18]
- Notice how their body changes. Do they:

  - Squirm with embarrassment?
  - Return your smile?
  - Burst into laughter?
  - Reach out and touch you back?
  - Nod their head and thank you for saying what you did?
  - Soften and relax their body momentarily?

18

8 Are You Listening to Me?

Few things are more disheartening than pouring your heart out to someone, only to look up and find that their eyes have glazed over and they are doing their best to stifle a yawn. The realisation that they are bored and uninterested in something that is of huge personal importance to you is humiliating and more often than not makes you want to retreat quickly back into your solitary shell, so as never to suffer the same ignominious experience again.

However, there is an art to gaining and maintaining another person's attention, and it is one that, with practice, can be learnt. In this chapter we are going to look at how you can acquire some of the body language skills that make people sit up and listen. Some of the situations in which you might want to use these skills include:

- Talking on a one-to-one basis[1]
- Talking with a group of friends
- Giving a speech
- Leading a group[2]
- Giving instructions or information
- Teaching
- Talking to a child

Signs of attention – or lack of it

In order to speak effectively, it is essential to be able to spot whether or not you have the attention of the person or group you are speaking to. There are several body language signals that will clue you in.

Personal space

Contrary to what you might expect, the proximity of the person is not necessarily significant to how much attention they are paying.[3] If your communication skills are good, you can effectively reach a person who is quite far away from you. For example, if you are giving a speech, a person sitting at the back of the audience may be paying the utmost attention to what you are saying.[4] On another occasion, an eavesdropper sitting a couple of seats away from you on the local bus may hang on your every word.

Posture

Leaning the body forwards indicates keenness and enthusiasm to hear what is being said. Conversely, leaning the body backwards sends a distinct message that the listener would really like to remove or distance themselves from what is being said. Leaning backwards can also indicate aloofness and a sense of superiority.

Leaning backwards with the legs or ankles crossed and the hands held behind the head gives the message, 'I am not interested in what you have to say, as I know better than you'.[5] When confronted by this posture you are not going to make any impact whatsoever until the person shifts position. Try pouncing on them craftily with a question such as 'What is your opinion about it?'

Head positions

A forward tilted head indicates interest. Tilting the head to one side indicates that the person is absorbed in what is being said. If you want to give the impression of studious listening, then hold this position.[6]

Propping the head on the hand suggests severe boredom. It may even give the impression that if the hand was suddenly removed, the person would collapse into a welcome sleep.

Nodding the head at the end of sentences and at points of interest demonstrates interest and indicates that the gist of what is being said has been grasped.[7] Nodding the head is also a visual cue to encourage the other person to continue speaking. If a person is responding with encouraging positive words but is nevertheless looking away, they are displaying a pointed lack of interest.

Facial expressions

Smiling and reacting to what is being said shows appreciation and encouragement to the speaker to continue. Displaying obvious negative expressions while verbally disagreeing can have the effect of livening up a conversation by prompting spirited counter-opinions in response.

Eye signals

Lack of eye contact is an invariable signal that a person is not listening to what you are saying.[8] This is not to say, of course, that a listener will be looking you constantly in the eye – an experience that would probably be very uncomfortable. Good eye contact is always intermittent. When involved in a one-to-one conversation, we often look away as we recall thoughts and emotions. When the speaker comes to an important part in the conversation – usually towards the end of a sentence – they will generally establish eye contact once again.

Mouth expressions

Signs of positive attention include smiling and laughing.[9] On the other hand, while a yawn unmistakeably signals boredom.[10]

Hand gestures

If the hands are clasped behind the head, your listener has probably got bored.

Finger gestures

Drumming fingers or fiddling with fingers may indicate boredom and inattention.[11] If the chin is resting in the hand, with the finger pointing upwards the listener is contemplating what is being said.

If they are biting their nails with a quizzical look, they are uncertain.

Touching

If the listener is responding with touch – for example, patting your back if you need comfort or lightly slapping your arm in response to a joke – you have their full attention.

Leg gestures

Barrier gestures (see pages 86–7) are a sure sign that your listener has put up their defences and is no longer paying attention. If they are pointing their foot towards you, on the other hand, they are likely to be interested in what you are saying.

Props

Fiddling with objects such as jewellery or mobile phones suggests a lack of interest (or perhaps undue nervousness).

How to respond to signs of boredom

It is very difficult to mask signs of boredom. The whole body slumps and energy seems to drain away.[12] If your companion, or audience, is showing signs of boredom, you need to act quickly to restore their attention.

If you want to make sure that a person listens to something vitally important, hold your hands firmly on their shoulders and maintain eye contact until you have said what you need to say. If you are aware that you have lost their attention, try changing your body posture dramatically, for example by turning your back on them.

If you are speaking to a large group, try using flamboyant arm gestures, as these help to attract attention even at a distance and serve to focus your audience.[13] Sweeping arm movements will, incidentally, also help you to breathe more deeply and freely, which will in turn help you to project yourself more openly and confidently.

In a large group situation also make sure you ask that everyone switches off their mobile phone before you start speaking.

If you feel you have lost the attention of an audience, try taking your jacket off or pausing for a sip of water. Alternatively, stop talking and do not start again until everyone is looking at you once again.

Interjecting

I think it is totally acceptable to let someone know if they have told you a story before.[14] You can interject politely by using a palm-up stop sign and saying, 'Yes, I remember you told me that before.' This lets them know you were listening the first time around, saves them repeating themselves and saves you getting bored. You also avoid the embarrassment of trying to feign interest – which will probably look unconvincing and alienate the speaker.

15 Exercise: Nodding

Experiment with nodding in the following way during conversation or when giving or receiving information.[15]

- When someone gives you eye contact, do not nod in response.
- Notice whether they are inclined to end the conversation or change the subject.
- Now make sure you nod your head at every cue and see if this encourages the speaker to talk at greater length.

This simple exercise will show you how positive feedback helps the other person to feel confident about what they are saying and encourages them to go on speaking.

   The ability to maintain a person's attention is a natural born skill to a fortunate few; luckily for the rest of us, it is also an art that can be developed with practice.[16] Good eye contact and an erect body posture are the keys to it; a consciousness of these body language skills will help to ensure that people sit up and take notice of you.

16

9 Who's Stressed Out?

Modern-day living has become increasingly fast-paced and time is always at a premium. Our Western society is also becoming more and more competitive. As expectations rise, we are burdened with higher and higher demands and mounting pressure. Our work and social diaries are often full, and we strive to squeeze more and more activities into each day. In general, we are working harder and for longer in order to live comfortably and enjoy what social and recreational time our busy schedules allow us. The end of the working day often finds us exhausted.[2] If we are lucky, we are able to take the occasional holiday, a brief respite from the escalating pressures of our working lives, and a chance to recuperate.

A certain amount of stress is actually a motivational factor in our daily lives, but the line between positive stress and unhealthy pressure is a fine one. Stress is, indirectly, one of biggest killers in our society, and it can manifest itself in a myriad of ways – headaches or migraine, panic attacks, asthma, high blood pressure, stomach ulcers, heart disease, strokes, heart attacks and many forms of cancer.

High levels of stress are associated with commonplace situations such as divorce, death, moving house and taking out a financial loan.[1] Having to deal with two or more of these stressful situations within a time frame of 18 months has been shown often to have a serious adverse effect on our health. But what really makes a difference to our stress levels is attitude, because stress is really all about how we react to and deal with the issues that confront us.

3

Thinking positively, meditating, taking exercise and learning to relax are all helpful tools in reducing stress. Accepting who we are and expressing ourselves freely and assertively, while allowing others the same privilege, are also likely to make our lives that little bit more stress-free.

What happens to the body under stress?

When we are under stress – whether because we are taking an exam, making a speech, working to meet a deadline, worried about a failing relationship, waiting for important news or whatever – our body undergoes a series of physiological reactions. These include:

- Pallor in the face, then fluctuating between pallor and flushing[3]
- A rush of adrenaline into the circulatory system, speeding it up[4]
- An increase in heart rate
- An increase in blood supply to the muscles and the brain
- The slowing of digestion
- An increase in blood sugar levels
- Dilation of the pupils
- An increase in breathing rate, filling the lungs with extra oxygen
- An increase in sweating[5]
- Dryness in the mouth[6]

4

5

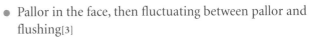

6

The body language of stress

An awareness of the physical changes that occur within our own bodies when we are stressed out can help us to keep a regular check on our personal well-being. Effective measures for combating stress build-up include:

- Taking time out
- Learning to relax the body – and, more importantly, the mind
- Taking regular exercise to provide the lungs with fresh clean air and raise the heart rate

Being aware of the symptoms of stress in others can also help us to be more compassionate and understanding, while on a practical note we can take measures to help them. Supportive body language includes reaching out and touching the stressed person, offering them a smile and even massaging out some of the knots of tension that build up around the base of the neck.[7]

Personal space

When we are stressed we extend our personal space zone and become extra sensitive to anyone entering it. If you are dealing with someone who is under stress, the safest bet is to maintain a generous distance and enter their personal space only when encouraged to do so.

8

9

10

Posture

A stressed body is agitated and restless due to the effects of adrenaline, which makes it ready for action.

Head positions

Head movements may be swift, jerky and over-reactive to any external stimuli. Another common position is the head slumped forward and supported by one or two hands, implying exhaustion and resignation.[8]

Facial expressions

When under stress we can become so absorbed with our own issues that we give the appearance of being in our own private world, and our facial expressions mirror this. We might grind our teeth, for example.[9] They may appear extreme, exaggerated, over-reactive or withdrawn.

Eye signals

When we are in a highly stressed state, our pupils become very dilated. Eye movements can be swift and rapid and at other times static and unfocused, as if we are staring vacantly into space.[10]

Watch out for eye cut-off signals, in which a person closes the eyes briefly. This movement calms the brain by cutting out all outside stimuli. A person who is using eye cut-off signals will be unable to engage fully in conversation, however politely they appear to be replying verbally. Bear in mind that this eye signal is merely a visual manifestation of stress and a need for withdrawal rather than an intentional slight directed at us.

Mouth expressions

Tension can sometimes manifest itself in a tight jaw and the grinding of teeth, especially while asleep. Periodically through the day, check for tension in your jaw and attempt to relax the muscles around your mouth if you realise that it has indeed tensed up.

Hand gestures

Hand gestures can be erratic and highly energised. Wringing of the hands expresses severe distress. Slapping our own hand, even in fun, is a negative gesture and one that suggests the desire to be punished.

Finger gestures

Stress is often expressed in a drumming of the fingers, as if we are impatient. Erratic, compulsive twitchy movements suggest nervousness and agitation, as does fiddling absent-mindedly with your hair or with inanimate objects.[11]

Touching

As we withdraw into our own world we begin to withhold touching gestures to others. Self-supportive gestures increase in frequency, as we try to hold ourselves together. We may pat ourselves in an attempt to offer self-support or wrap our arms around our body.[12] We may huddle up into the foetal position for comfort and the exclusion of others.[13] Other signals include biting our nails, and even sucking our thumb or touching ourselves sexually for comfort and relief.

Arm gestures

When under stress we tend to protect ourselves by hiding behind defensive arm barriers. We may also wrap our arms around ourselves to offer ourselves comfort. Wrapping our arms around our legs and resting our head on our knees is a comforting, cocooned foetal gesture.[14]

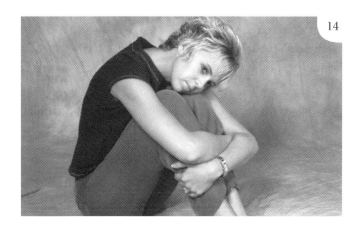

15

Leg gestures

Foot-tapping and leg-shaking are unconscious nervous actions that express agitation and impatience.

Stress and a tip on timing

If you are feeling stressed, try to slow down your body movements. This is something that happens naturally when we are feeling calm, and by mimicking this process it is possible to increase your feeling of calm.[15] Try this technique, too, if you are dealing with another person who is stressed. Your more relaxed pace will encourage them to slow down, and, hopefully, therefore calm down.

Exercise: Count to ten

16

This is a body-language-oriented take on a simple old-fashioned but very effective exercise to calm an agitated mind: breathe and count to ten. If you make the effort to do this exercise, the benefits will soon become obvious.

- Next time you are feeling stressed or agitated, take yourself off to a quiet place – if you are at work, lock yourself in the toilet (next to an open window if possible, as you should ideally be breathing in fresh air).
- Stand erect – head up, shoulders back – and place one hand on your solar plexus (slightly above your belly button) or on your hips.[16]
- Take a slow deep breath through your nose, keeping your shoulders still. Allow the breath to travel deep down into your belly and pelvic region. Feel your hand rise as the air enters your lower body.
- Hold the breath for a moment and then release it slowly, noticing the fall of your hand as you do so.

When you have exhaled almost completely, expel the last drop of air by puffing out with your lips.

Repeat these steps ten times – or more if you are able – each time concentrating absolutely on the journey of each breath as it enters and leaves your body. After ten breaths your stress level will be greatly reduced.

Being stressed is a condition that comes gradually upon us, while we are hardly aware of it happening. There are times when most of us drive our minds and our bodies beyond their normal sphere of endurance, in the unrealistic hope that at some point soon there will be time to relax – which, of course, when we take this attitude, there never is. And if we do eventually achieve a long-awaited holiday, we are often too exhausted to enjoy the break. An awareness of the body language in this chapter will help you to notice when you are on the slippery slope to maximum stress and enable you to do something about it – by respecting your body's need for regular food, rest and exercise.[17]

17

10 So Who's Lying?

1

Human nature is such that we rarely challenge a liar, even when their words are clearly untrue. Instead, we find a polite way to end the conversation – or we happily listen to what is being said while trying to remember as much as possible so we can repeat it later for our own entertainment. Often we have no direct evidence that a person is lying, but we pick it up subconsciously through their body language. We may feel suspicious or simply uncomfortable in their presence.

Of course, there are situations where telling a lie is seen as the most socially acceptable thing to do. A white lie spares people's feelings and causes harm to no one. Some would say that it is altruistic. Often both parties are complicit in the telling of a white lie. Imagine, for example that you are at a party and are not enjoying yourself. Your host sees that something is wrong and comes over to ask you if you are having a good time. You reply that you are having a terrific time and it's a wonderful party.[1]

Why we can't help giving ourselves away

2

Scientific research shows that even the most accomplished of liars cannot control the automatic or reflex reactions that occur within the body when we tell a lie. Lying creates stress, which can range from a slight tension to an intense fear. Our blood pressure and pulse rate rise, our breathing patterns change and our face may become pale as the blood is drained away.[2] Stress affects the digestive juices, causing the stomach to churn. In extreme cases, this may be accompanied by swift and violent bowel movements. Blushing and sweating can also occur in inexperienced liars.

3

The nose touch

An accomplished and experienced liar will be able, to a large extent, to disguise many of the signs of lying. One sign that is often overlooked, however, is the irresistible urge to scratch or rub the nose.[3] There is a physiological reason for this urge. When a person tells a lie, stress initially causes the blood to drain from their face, giving them a pale complexion. This is followed by an excessive flow of blood to the facial vessels, congesting around the nasal area, which causes the nose to itch and the liar to scratch. During Bill Clinton's famous interrogation regarding the nature of his relationship with Monica Lewinksky, he was observed to scratch his nose more than 25 times.

It is important to note that the nose touch also occurs when our words do not concur with our inner thoughts, which cannot accurately be described as lying. A person in turmoil and uncertainty may struggle to find the appropriate words and may touch their nose while striving to rephrase internally what they are about to say. While they are not intending to deceive, it would be fair to say that they are not saying what they are thinking.

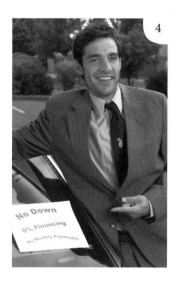

4

When you might need to spot a lie

Of course, there are situations in which it is preferable to let a harmless lie pass. At other times, however, it is important to be able to detect whether or not you are being told the truth.[4]

Personal relationships

Within our personal relationships we all tell white lies. Perhaps you tell your partner the new dress cost just a bit less than it did.[5] Many of these are for our own self-protection and personal privacy, and for the protection of those that we love. Even within a marriage there are many issues that are not discussed and many things that are better left unsaid. Past relationships are always a difficult area, a topic that can bring up uncomfortable, negative emotions such as jealousy and insecurity for both parties.

Nevertheless, there are moments when it is imperative to know whether you are being lied to. Fidelity is the big one here. Though it may be easier to believe that everything is okay, there comes a moment when we need to confront the truth in order to reach a realistic resolution.

Children and teenagers

Good parenting teaches children right from wrong, and a child who deliberately lies warrants a sensitive investigation. Fear of punishment is usually the cause of this behaviour.[6]

In adolescence, teenagers often become secretive in order to distance themselves from their parents.[7] Telling a probing mum or dad what they want to hear rather than the truth may be a way to appease them and minimise confrontation.

Social situations

Armed with a little knowledge, observing people in social situations can be a great source of fun and entertainment. This is especially so when your subjects exaggerate and deliberately fabricate in order to impress and gain admiration.

In professional situations

Blatant falsehoods are relatively rare within the professional environment, as in time they are likely to be discovered, and when this happens, dire consequences will usually result.[9]

The consumer, on the other hand, often falls prey to professional deception. The rogue tradesman, the insurance company that sells you insurance you do not require, the plumber who charges for parts you do not need or labour he did not do, the car salesman who knowingly sells you a faulty second-hand car ... the list of possible deceptions is endless. Familiarising yourself with the body language of lying can be an invaluable tool when you are dealing with sellers, providers, agents, tradespeople and so on.

Spotting lies on TV

Live television shows can be an invaluable source for the study of body language. Chat shows are particularly good because camera shots often include the whole body. This means that you can observe the whole array of body gestures in real time. You will frequently observe such scenes as the chat show host rubbing his nose while saying something along the lines of, 'I saw your show and I thought it was fabulous.'

Politicians are another fascinating source of TV entertainment where lying is concerned.[8] They are trained in the use of body language, and in order to avoid giving themselves away with it will cleverly place themselves behind tables and desks or tightly hold on to a document.

Show you are telling the truth

To show you are being truthful, keep your body relaxed and your body language open, ensuring there are no defensive barriers between you and the person you are talking to (see pages 86–8). Remember to breathe deeply, and if possible have both feet planted firmly on the ground.

Moving – sensitively – into the other person's personal space will also help give credibility to what you are saying, even more so if you are able to reach out and touch them. A supportive hand expresses solidity as well as making a personal intimate contact. Speak directly to the person as you touch them and establish good eye contact.[10] If the other person is looking away, do not speak until they make eye contact, and if necessary ask them to look at you. Once you have said what you need to say, maintain eye contact and give a slight nod of your head. This will encourage them to respond to you in an affirmative manner.

You cannot make someone believe you if they are stubbornly intent on disbelieving, but it is worth remembering that actions speak louder than words. Your behaviour is far more important than what you have to say when you are trying to establish credibility.

10

The body language of deceit

Deceit (for whatever reason) takes practice to perfect – and it is very possible to become accomplished at the art of lying. Actors, for example, who spend the majority of their working time portraying feelings that are not their own, may practise deceit very skilfully, should they wish to, in their own lives. Politicians, too, have many opportunities to exercise the skill of deception. Without this kind of practice, however, for most of us – particularly if we seldom have cause to deceive – telling a lie is psychologically excruciatingly uncomfortable and physically very difficult to do effectively.

Posture

To help us create more of a distance, when we are lying, we unconsciously lean slightly backwards. The saying 'squirming in your seat' suggests that lying causes such discomfort that the natural impulse when telling a lie is to get away.[11]

Head positions

If we are lying, looking directly at a person and holding eye contact is a difficult thing to do. We naturally want to turn our head away so that the other person cannot see our face. If a person is trying to avoid this give-away trait, their body and head may become unnaturally rigid and their movements and expressions minimal. This body language is often observable in television interviews and political speeches, particularly if the politician is defending him or herself from some unsavoury allegations. It might be described as a bare-faced lie.

Facial expressions

When the words spoken do not tally with the facial expression, you can be pretty sure that the speaker is lying. Always believe the face rather than the words. When telling a lie, we often grimace involuntarily, especially when talking about something unpalatable, and may also blush.[12]

Eye signals

Shifty eyes reflect a guilty discomfort, as does the attempt to minimise eye contact.[13] Closing the eyes and blinking more than is natural is a cut-off signal, expressing a desire to escape from the discomfort felt in the current situation, even though the relief is only for a brief moment. Beady eyes express displeasure and disdain. Staring eyes are aggressively attempting to coerce you into believing what is being said.

Exercise: Shifty eyes

This is an eye observation exercise. It will enable you to determine in which direction a person tends to shift their eyes when telling the truth and, conversely, when being deceitful.

- In normal conversation ask an acquaintance a routine question that you know the answer to.
- Observe in which horizontal direction they shift their eyes as they look downwards to prepare a truthful answer. You now know which way their eyes shift when they are telling the truth.[14]
- Now ask a question to which you feel they might be tempted to respond untruthfully.
- Observe whether their eyes shift in the same or a different direction. If they shift in a different direction, it is highly likely that this person is indeed being untruthful.[15]

14

15

16

Mouth expressions

A child telling a lie will instinctively try to cover the whole of the mouth to mask the falsehood. As adults we still have the same innate desire, but we find more discreet ways of expressing it. We lift the hand towards the mouth and may touch the cheek or the chin, or find an area to scratch or rub. The mouth also becomes drier as a result of the tension created by being deceitful, and we may want to take a drink or swallow hard in order to lubricate it.[16] If we are especially tense about a lie, our lips may quiver when we speak and tight jaw muscles may be evident.[17]

Hand gestures

A common gesture when telling a lie is the open-palmed hand and shoulder shrug. The shoulders hunch up briefly as the palms of the hand turn outward, then just as quickly the shoulders drop back and the position of the hands returns to normal.[18] This suggests a momentary feeling of helplessness and an almost resigned apology for lying. The stereotypical hard-faced second-hand car salesman, may use a similar gesture, akin to a prolonged open-palmed hand plea. This is in fact a passive-aggressive ploy, imploring you to quickly accept what is being said as the truth. A shaking hand is letting out nervous energy and is clearly showing signs of stress. This is also often the case with any kind of finger tapping or twiddling.

17

In an attempt to 'speak no evil' the hand will often discreetly touch a spot around the mouth area, in an attempt to 'hear no evil' it will pull or tug at the ear, and in an attempt to 'see no evil' it will rub the eye or an area around the eye. Watch out especially for the ubiquitous nose touch, which is the most prevalent gesture used when lying (see page 162).

18

Body contact

As lying to another person is an uncomfortable experience, body contact is generally avoided. Be aware, however, that a skilled deceiver may deliberately make body contact in order to appear more convincing.[19] As a rule, let your gut instinct be your guide.

Arm gestures

Watch out for contradictory body gestures. If a person is agreeing with you verbally while at the same time exhibiting defensive arm barriers (see pages 86–7), they are unlikely to be telling the whole truth.[21]

Leg gestures

When a person is ensconced behind a desk, counter or witness stand, many strong visual signs of lying are conveniently hidden from view. Foot-tapping, foot-twitching and foot jerks are all signals that a person is not being honest.[20] The foot twitch is my own personal give-away signal. I am expert at maintaining the appropriate facial expression and am able to refrain from all other tell-tale gestures, but I cannot stop my foot from making an upward jerking movement.

22

Clothes

The discomfort of lying makes us hot, and we may loosen our clothes as a result. Picking imaginary lint from our clothing is a common distraction gesture and a sign of unease.[22]

For most of us, deception does not come easy, as the body automatically strives to give us away. Concealing the automatic body responses takes an enormous amount of effort. In fact, the only way to master the art of deception 100 per cent is to completely believe in your own lie!

11 You and Whose Army?

For many members of the animal kingdom, survival depends on having a body that is equipped either for killing or for self-protection. The success of the human species, however, depends as much on our mental attributes as our physical prowess. The human body is certainly not well equipped for physical combat. We walk on two legs, thus exposing our neck and all our vital organs. We run relatively slowly. The surface of our body is covered not by fur or hide but by a relatively delicate layer of skin. We have neither sharp teeth nor long claws.[1] We have compensated for our physical lack by using our brain to develop weapons and all manner of devious methods – such as knives, guns and the weapons of germ warfare – to kill and cause pain to other people.

However, anger can be used in a far more effective and constructive way if it is channelled into the clever use of words and body language. Evasive action such as turning your back on an aggressor and simply walking away is often the most positive way to deal with a threatening situation.[2]

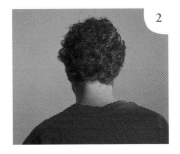

Meeting aggressive body language

The instances in which aggressive body language can occur are legion. The following are a just few examples of situations where you may come up against it:

- Family confrontations
- Protection of property
- Disputes with neighbours[3]
- On the road[4]
- At work
- Competitive situations
- Sporting events such as football matches
- Social situations, especially where alcohol is present

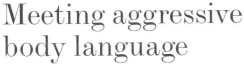

5

6

How to avoid giving an aggressive response

If you are angry and feeling aggressive towards another person or feel like insulting them, at all costs avoid reacting physically – otherwise you will only regret it later. Even if they are threatening you physically, try to remain calm.[5] Firing back an insult or an insulting gesture is almost as bad: an insult is simply an indirect act of aggression. Remember the old saying and count to ten; count to 100 if you have to. In such a situation, responding hastily is self-destructive.

Take a step back and move away if possible. Take some deep breaths and regain your composure. Firmly grip hold of some nearby object – hold your own hand if nothing else is available – and release any pent-up tension with a firm squeeze. If you are then feeling calm – and only if you are feeling calm – speak to the other person, choosing your words with care and making sure you use 'I' statements such as 'I feel small when you say that' rather than 'You make me feel small.'[6] Own your own feelings and try to express them calmly, clearly and assertively.

How to defuse potentially aggressive situations

If you are faced with a potentially aggressive or violent situation, the most useful thing you can do is get out of the way as quickly as possible, removing yourself and your loved ones to a place of safety. This is equally true of a road-rage situation as an explosive board meeting.[7] That being said, people do perform deeds of great heroism and have been known to accomplish physical feats that are almost impossible to believe. This has been explained by the surge of adrenaline triggered by fear. In 1982 Margaret Baker, a housewife from Pennsylvania, USA, reportedly saved her child from being crushed to death by a car that had been turned over by a group of violent protestors. She lifted the car off the screaming child by brute force alone – a feat that ought to have been impossible.

The natural instinct when confronted with a violent aggressor is to cower, bending the knees and holding the arm over the face and head to protect it from injury.[8] This position makes you look small and helpless and tells the aggressor that you do not intend to confront him or her. To show that you have no interest whatsoever in being involved, you can try folding your arms, crossing your legs, bending your body over and lowering your head – a posture of ultimate defensiveness. You should also avoid all eye contact.

A more courageous ploy would be to lean slightly forward into the aggressor's space, bow your head forward and look the aggressor in the eye while speaking to them about whatever the issue is. To do this you need to be able to relax your body while you are under threat and frightened, which is a difficult thing to do. However, if you can manage it, it can prove a helpful tactic, as most bullies are cowards.

9

The body language of aggression

We all have to face aggression at moments in our life, and it is an inevitable fact that most of us will, in the heat of the moment, behave aggressively to another person at least on a few occasions. A knowledge of the body language of aggression can help you to deal more effectively with such a situation when it arises – whether you are on the receiving end or have yourself let your anger get out of hand.

10

Personal space

A person who is behaving aggressively will intrude on your personal space, touching your possessions and possibly even parts of your body in an effort to provoke you. They may also attempt to block or restrict your movements, for example by placing their body in front of yours if you make to leave.

Posture

Making oneself appear as tall as possible while shrugging the shoulders in a forward rotating movement is an intimidating gesture and implies preparation for physical action.[9] Standing firm with legs apart suggests lack of fear. The old-fashioned ready-for-action stance is the boxing position, with knees bent, one leg placed behind the other, and hands in fists placed at a diagonal angle to the legs. The eyebrows are furrowed to create an intimidating and serious expression. These days, however, bare-knuckle fighting is rare, and we are more likely to come across the more intimidating spectacle of a knife held in a menacing manner.

Head positions

Jutting the head forwards and backwards in a rhythmic fashion is a threatening gesture. The jaw may also be thrust forward, goading the other person into action.[10]

Facial expressions

A false half-smile indicates covert aggression. Baring the teeth gives a more obviously aggressive message.[11] A noticeable pallor suggests that a person is in an alert, nervous state and is highly likely to make an attack. This is a sign of a very dangerous situation.

Eye expressions

Direct eye contact can be used to challenge. Rapid eye movements suggest nervousness, fear and possible drug abuse. Dilation of the pupils may also be drug related. If you are confronted by an aggressor, try to avert your eyes and avoid any eye contact.

Mouth expressions

Aggressive mouth expressions include spitting and tongue movements mimicking a fast licking performed in a sexual fashion. Gulping and an obvious difficulty in breathing suggest a highly nervous person in a severe state of tension.

Hand gestures

Fist shaking is certainly a sign of a person who is angry but does not imply that this person is likely to make aggressive contact.[12] When two hands are thrust forward, making a gesture suggestive of wringing the neck or throttling, anger and aggression are clearly indicated.[13] Hands on the hips accompanied by a stern facial expression suggest anger. The slow hand clap can be used as a derogatory gesture implying disgust and disdain.

A hand placed on the brow, over the closed eyes, can suggest a 'had it up to here' feeling, indicating that toleration limits have been reached.[14]

15

Finger gestures

The fingers can be very expressive in suggesting anger and are often used to give insults. The V sign is probably the best known of these. In this gesture the index finger and middle finger face towards the body in a V-shape and are moved swiftly upwards in a motion directed at the victim. A more modern equivalent is the upward-pointing middle finger.

Stabbing and pointing the index finger are sure signs of anger. If either of them is accompanied by the aggressor moving towards you and repeating the gesture, move out of the way fast!

The finger wag is a gesture of reprimand in which the finger points away from the body and moves from side to side.[15]

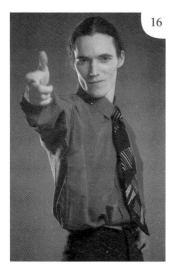

16

The shooting gesture is made with the index finger and middle finger held together in a gun-like shape. The fingers point towards the victim.[16]

The two-finger eye jab is suggestive of poking the eyes out. The index finger and middle finger are held open side by side and the hand is thrust forwards as if to gouge out the offending person's eyes.

The throat slit is done by sliding the index finger against your own throat. However, the gesture is actually directed at another person, indicating that they are 'in for it' – or, metaphorically, about to get their throat cut.

17

The thumb send off is a sure sign that whoever you have angered has had enough and wishes you out of the way.[17] The hand forms a fist with the thumb held upwards and thrust repeatedly over the shoulder, indicating that you should leave at once.

Touching

Physically pushing or shoving another person out of the way with the hands is, of course, a gesture of anger and/or retaliation.[18] Any unwanted hands-on contact can be construed as an aggressive act. When this contact is sexual in intent – and particularly if it involves intimate areas such as the breast, bottom, inner thigh or genitalia – it is very abusive.

Arm gestures

We instinctively defend ourselves by using our hands and arms to fend off any blow that is coming towards us.[19]

While venting our anger or giving someone a piece of our mind, we often stand with our arms wrapped around us. This protective gesture gives us support and helps us to feel guarded while we tell someone an uncomfortable truth. Arms are also weapons that we use to lash out at others when we cannot control our anger.

Leg gestures

Kicking is, of course, an aggressive act. We also kick out our legs into the air as an expression and release of our anger.

Clothes

Certain gangs and subcultures purposely adopt intimidating clothing – for example the Hell's Angels, skinheads and Goths.[20] When gathered *en masse* they can certainly make an impact, regardless of whether they have any aggressive intention. Indeed, any large gathering of people 'in uniform' can feel threatening. Finding oneself in the company of a group of football supporters, for example, can be a terrifying experience. Wearing such a 'uniform' makes a statement of solidarity with the group, its beliefs and its ideals.

Exercise: Body mirroring to reduce conflict

Next time you are in the unfortunate situation of having a disagreement with someone, try defusing a potential argument by using this tactic.

- Always try to remain calm.[21]
- Position yourself opposite and directly in front of the other person – at arm's length is a perfect and safe distance.
- Mirror the other person's body language: if they are standing, stand; if they are sitting, then sit down too.
- Let them say what they have to say, listen to their argument and simply agree with them.

With any luck the argument will be forgotten, as this exercise often results in both parties bursting into laughter.

In inner-cities these days everyone is accustomed to noise. Sadly, the result is that if you have to scream or call for help in a threatening situation, you are likely to be ignored. If we hear a scream in the street outside, most of us find it convenient to assume that it is in jest – horseplay by late-night revellers – and remain in the safety of our own homes. If ever you are in immediate danger and desperately in need of help, the most effective word to scream at the top of your voice is 'FIRE!' This will alert even the deafest of ears and will trigger a widespread response. Even if only out of curiosity or because they are worried that they are themselves in danger, most people will come running to find out what is going on.

21

Remember that violence affects a small number of people; be sensible and cautious but don't let irrational fears make you over-concerned. Although statistically women are at less risk of becoming the victims of street violence than men, nevertheless women tend to feel more vulnerable than men when travelling alone. If you do find yourself face to face with an adversary (and, of course, these strategies can also be used by men), try the following:

22

- Avoid eye contact, totally blanking them – perhaps by switching your attention to some object that you happen to be carrying.[22]
- Pretend to make a call on your mobile phone (even if there is no signal), clearly stating where you are and confirming loudly that the person on the other end of the line is about to meet you.[23] (I always make a point of calling home when travelling in a taxi late at night and often end up telling the answering machine where I am and when to expect me.)
- Lower your voice and try to sound calm and in control.
- Tell the aggressor that you have seen them before and know their identity.
- Be sympathetic rather than confrontational.
- If you are a woman and are being sexually threatened by a man, it may be worth an attempt at appealing to his morals. If all else fails, my advice would be to kick him in the goollies and run for it!

23

24

In hostage situations, befriending your aggressor is said to be your best plan of action and diminishes the likelihood of assault against you.

A large percentage of the aggressive behaviour in our world today is due to alcohol and – to a lesser extent – drug abuse.[24] Dealing with a person who is under the influence of alcohol is far more straightforward than dealing with a person who has been taking drugs, as their behaviour is somewhat predictable. They may be verbally abusive but are rarely fast on their feet, and their mental agility is greatly impaired. It is relatively easy to remove yourself from their company. Drug-related violence may be a consequence of attempts to steal money to feed the habit. Many drugs do not predispose the taker to violence.

We all have a certain amount of aggression in our system; this is normal and natural and is only a problem if we lose control – in which case anger can become a negative and destructive emotion. Aggression can be a positive and creative energy if channelled into labour-intensive chores, such as chopping wood, or artistic pursuits, such as making music or artwork.

And finally ... remember that violent aggressive acts are rare. Don't allow your fear of them to get out of proportion.

12 Do As I Do – and As I Say

For all of us there are times when we say things that are not strictly true. This does not mean we are guilty of telling outright lies. There are many situations in which etiquette, tact, diplomacy or threat call for us to say the right thing at the right time, even though it may not be what we really mean.

There is a saying, 'Actions speak louder than words.' How true it is! At a subconscious level we are always reading and interpreting the body language of others. If a person tells us one thing in words and something else with their body, we immediately register the discrepancy, even if we have no formal knowledge of body language whatsoever. Someone who says 'Yes, do come in for coffee' with their arms folded and eyes raised probably wants you anywhere but in their kitchen.[1] Although we may not immediately be able to put our finger on it, we will invariably conclude that something here is not quite right. We may call this a hunch or gut instinct, but in fact we are assessing and assimilating the body language we are seeing and instinctively know that it is conflicting with the words we are hearing.

Take, for example, a woman who feels that there is something amiss with her marriage. Over a period of time she comes to the conclusion that her husband is having an affair. What makes her sense this? She looks for confirmation that all is well by asking her husband, 'Do you love me?' Even after he has given her the verbal reassurance she needs, however, she still feels uneasy.[2] This is because the way her partner is acting does not match what he is saying. He used to make a point of coming over to cuddle her, and that

doesn't happen any more. He has started buying her flowers, but when he gives them to her there is no twinkle or laughter in his eyes. In fact he doesn't look into her eyes at all any more. When she reaches out to initiate a cuddle, she notices that his body recoils from her touch. It is only for a split second but it is there. When she tries to engage him in conversation, he is uneasy about looking her in the eye and either makes an excuse to leave the room or occupies himself with some activity such as making a drink – anything to distance himself physically from her. Even in his sleep he turns his back on her, pretending to be asleep if she puts out an arm to hold or hug him.

Let's consider a few situations in which contradictory verbal and non-verbal messages are being given out.

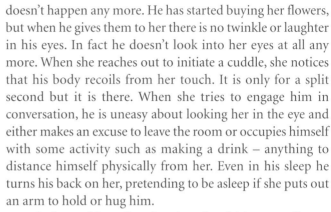

At work

An employee is to be reprimanded for inefficiency.[3] His employer asks him to come into the office. After the dressing-down, the employee apologises, holds his head down in acknowledgement of his shortfall and apologises for what he knows to be true. He gives the appearance of being humble and contrite as he professes that he will make up for his under-achievement.[4] However, the rest of his body is telling another story. In his pockets his fists are clenched, and under the desk his feet are making small kicking movements. His whole body is tense, and he appears to be flexing the muscles around his mouth and jaw. The truth is that the employee hates both his job and his boss, and is just biding his time while he waits to hear whether he has succeeded in getting another job he has just applied for.[5]

At school

A child is being bullied. Confronted by an older child, he is frightened of being physically hurt and backs away. He is shaking inside and tears are streaming down his face. However, he decides to take a stand. He shouts at the bullies aggressively, warning them that he is going to tell his big brother and he will deal with them. Though his verbal language is courageous, his body language communicates his real feeling of terror.[6]

6

In the doctor's surgery

A doctor's receptionist is speaking on the phone to a distressed caller. She responds with the appropriate sympathetic language and gives a good impression of being attentive. All the while, however, her body is slumped forward and she is doodling on the pad in front of her, although she appears not to notice what she is drawing, for her eyes have a glazed look and she is staring into space – except for the brief second when she looks at the clock over the surgery door. Similarly, a teacher might appear to be giving the class his whole attention but sneaking a look at his watch.[7]

7

At the shops

On my first visit to America I was at first delighted and later bemused by the attitude of retail assistants as I wondered around the shopping malls. I would invariably be asked quite pleasantly, 'How are you today?' as I entered and browsed around each store. I was so impressed by the beaming smiles and open, friendly body language of these shop assistants that I would promptly tell them exactly how I was doing and would chat away as if I had known them for years.

8

It didn't take me very long to notice the quizzical and bemused look that appeared on their faces as I chattered on. Evidently, they didn't actually expect a reply to their polite question, and if one was delivered, it was certainly not listened to. They had been well trained in the body language of politeness and friendliness, but it was apparent that no one had ever told them to mean what they are saying or to listen to a reply when given.[8]

9

My British sense of humour eventually took over. When I was greeted with, 'Good morning! How are you today?' I would make up the most absurd replies, knowing that the salesperson was not paying attention. I told them that my haemorrhoids were playing up badly this morning, that I had caught my husband making love to the cleaning lady, that I had found out I only had a few hours to live and so forth. There was never any response whatsoever, as they had not listened to a single word. As I left, they would tell me impeccably to 'Have a nice day', even though I might have just told them very clearly that I was being executed by a firing squad in the afternoon.

Avoiding mixed messages

10

There are many occasions throughout our lives that call for us to be polite, charming, courteous, courageous and sensitive to other people, regardless of our true inner feelings.[9] Wearing our heart on our sleeve all of the time would, after all, be impractical and exhausting for everyone concerned.

Most of us are adept at maintaining the composure of our face while attempting to conceal our inner feelings. We can maintain appropriate eye contact and make appropriate facial expressions while concealing quite contradictory feelings.[10] We concentrate our efforts on the face because this is the main area people focus on when they are communicating with us. However, we may not be quite so in charge of what the rest of our body is saying. Our lower body gestures often give away vital clues to the truth. Consider the following example:

You are just about the leave the office when someone calls you back. You make a grimace, but as you turn the top half of your body around, you quickly change your facial expression.[11] You smile, giving a good impression of calmness, serenity and interest in what they have to say. Your feet, however, are itching to get away and are still pointing towards the door; your hand remains steadfastly on the door handle. Below the neck you are clearly showing that you fully intend to leave the room.

When trying to decipher another person's true feelings and intentions, always look at their torso and lower body. From the way a person holds their torso it is possible to tell whether they are bored or excited.[12] Someone who is bored and tired will slump and relax their torso, whereas someone who is excited and energised will hold themselves upright and expand their chest. Check the legs for defensive barriers and look for toe-pointing pointers (see pages 87–8 and 134). The feet are generally the last body part to come under control and for me are always of great interest. A person who appears to be in command of themselves and in control of a situation can give themselves away by the slightest of foot gestures.

Television presenters are fascinating to watch in this respect. While they generally appear confident and interested in their guests, their foot gestures often reveal some very contradictory feelings. An upturned sole implies their discomfort and need to retreat. A rhythmically jerking foot suggests that they are sexually attracted to their guest. A sudden jerk with the foot implies that they are telling a lie, and foot tapping suggests that their guest has irritated them.

13

In conclusion

The study of body language is a fascinating and rewarding pastime.[13] An awareness of a just a few simple gestures that we all regularly use will enhance your powers of perception, fine-tune your intuition and give you more faith in your gut instinct about people.[14] You may notice that you become more confident when meeting new people and less intimidated by unfamiliar experiences. Watching the world go by can truly become a richer experience and a new adventure. You can learn to analyse your own communication skills, assess your weak and strong points, and then improve upon them, while adding new gestures to your repertoire.

I fervently hope that you spend some time experimenting with and gaining benefit from the information and exercises contained in these pages. This book is purposely designed to empower and enrich not only your body language but also your life. Good Luck!

14

Acknowledgements

Numbers refer to page/picture number.

©123rf
9/6, 10/10, 11/15, 12/16, 12/17, 14/21, 15/22, 15/23, 22/16, 27/30, 32/44, 35/3, 42/17, 46/30, 55/57, 55/59, 57/65, 59/68, 63/85, 68/104, 74/125, 82/17, 84/22, 97/11, 136/28, 142/4, 142/8, 143/10

©alamy
036/4, 43/21

©freeimages
064/88, 66/97, 66/99, 74/123, 81/15, 91/41, 91/42, 105/30, 105/32

©imagesource
011/13, 20/12, 24/21, 29/36, 29/37, 30/38, 33/45, 36/5, 37/8, 43/20, 65/92, 68/105, 68/107, 74/122, 124/32, 148/5, 162/3

©istock
009/8, 10/9, 13/19, 18/5, 22/15, 52/50, 95/8, 157/12

©library of congress
132/16

©Radius / SuperStock
10/12

©Robert Harding
42/16, 70/112

©stockexchange
7/1, 7/2, 8/3, 8/4, 8/5, 9/7, 10/11, 11/14, 13/18, 14/20, 17/1, 17/2, 17/3, 17/4, 18/6, 18/7, 19/8, 19/11, 20/13, 22/17, 23/18, 23/19, 23/20, 24/22, 25/23, 25/24, 25/25, 26/26, 26/27, 26/28, 26/29, 27/31, 28/32, 28/33, 28/34, 30/39, 30/40, 31/42, 32/33, 35/1, 36/6, 38/9, 38/10, 39/11, 41/15, 42/18, 44/23, 44/24, 44/25, 46/31, 47/33, 48/37, 48/38, 48/36, 49/40, 49/41, 49/42, 50/44, 52/49, 55/58, 56/61, 56/62, 57/63, 57/64, 58/66, 58/67, 60/73, 62/83, 64/90, 65/95, 66/98, 67/100, 67/101, 67/103, 69/108, 69/110, 71/114, 72/115, 72/116, 72/117, 73/119, 73/120, 74/124, 77/3, 78/4, 78/7, 79/8, 79/9, 79/10, 85/23, 90/40, 93/2, 93/3, 95/7, 96/9, 98/13, 100/20, 104/28, 112/49, 112/50, 113/1, 116/10, 117/13, 119/17, 120/21, 121/22, 122/27, 127/1, 127/2, 127/3, 128/6, 129/7, 130/10, 131/12, 131/14, 132/18, 133/20, 141/2, 145/16, 149/6, 150/10, 153/1, 154/3, 156/8, 157/13, 161/2, 163/7, 166/13, 171/2, 171/4, 177/19, 185/11

©superstock
62/82

©thinkstock

15/24, 33/46, 37/7, 39/12, 40/13, 40/14, 43/22, 46/29, 47/32, 47/34, 47/35, 48/39, 49/43, 50/45, 51/46, 51/47, 51/48, 53/51, 53/52, 53/53, 54/54, 54/55, 54/56, 59/69, 59/70, 59/71, 59/72, 60/74, 60/75, 60/76, 61/77, 61/78, 61/79, 62/81, 63/86, 64/91, 65/93, 65/94, 65/96, 67/102, 69/109, 70/111, 71/113, 72/118, 73/121, 75/126, 75/127, 75/128, 76/129, 76/130, 77/2, 78/6, 80/11, 80/12, 80/13, 81/14, 82/16, 83/18, 83/19, 83/20, 84/21, 85/24, 85/25, 86/26, 87/28, 88/30, 88/31, 88/32, 89/33, 89/34, 89/35, 89/36, 89/37, 90/38, 90/38, 90/39, 91/43, 91/44, 92/45, 92/46, 92/47, 93/1, 94/4, 94/5, 94/6, 96/10, 98/12, 98/14, 98/15, 99/16, 99/17, 99/18, 101/21, 101/22, 102/23, 102/24, 103/25, 103/26, 104/27, 106/33, 106/34, 106/35, 107/36, 107/37, 108/38, 108/39, 108/40, 109/42, 109/42, 110/44, 110/45, 111/46, 111/47, 111/48, 113/2, 113/3, 114/4, 114/5, 114/6, 115/7, 115/8, 115/9, 115/9, 116/11, 117/12, 117/14, 118/15, 118/16, 119/18, 119/19, 120/20, 121/23, 122/25, 122/26, 123/28, 124/30, 125/34, 125/35, 126/36, 126/37, 128/4, 128/5, 129/8, 130/9, 130/11, 131/13, 131/15, 132/17, 133/19, 133/21, 134/22, 134/24, 135/25, 135/26, 135/27, 136/29, 137/30, 137/31, 138/32, 138/33, 139/34, 139/35, 141/1, 141/3, 142/5, 142/6, 143/7, 144/11, 144/12, 144/13, 145/14, 145/15, 146/18, 147/1, 147/2, 148/3, 148/4, 149/8, 150/9, 150/11, 151/12, 151/13, 151/14, 152/15, 152/16, 153/2, 154/4, 154/5, 155/7, 156/9, 156/10, 157/11, 157/15, 158/16, 159/17, 162/4, 163/6, 164/8, 164/9, 165/10, 166/11, 166/12, 167/14, 167/15, 168/16, 168/17, 168/18, 169/19, 169/20, 169/21, 170/22, 171/1, 171/3, 172/5, 172/6, 173/7, 174/9, 174/10, 175/11, 175/12, 176/15, 176/16, 177/18, 178/21, 179/22, 179/23, 180/24, 181/1, 181/2, 182/3, 182/4, 182/5, 183/6, 183/7, 184/9, 184/10, 185/12, 186/13, 186/14

©ucl

19/9, 19/10, 64/89, 121/23, 173/8, 177/20

Anna Jaskolka

30/41, 61/80, 62/84, 63/87, 68/105, 86/27, 87/29, 124/31, 134/23, 143/9, 145/17, 154/6, 157/14, 161/1, 163/5, 175/13, 175/14, 176/17

Clipart

021/14

Jo St Mart

109/41

Wendy Hobson

29/35, 35/2, 42/19, 45/26, 45/27, 45/28, 56/60, 77/1, 78/5, 100/19, 105/29, 105/31, 123/29, 124/33, 149/7, 183/8

Cover

Front cover: top left © Superstock; bottom left © Fotolia; centre © Superstock; top right © Fotolia; bottom right © Stockexchange

Spine: © Superstock

Back cover: top © iStock; middle © iStock; bottom © Superstock

Index